CW00881512

Upon My Last Word of Honor

Upon My Last Word of Honor

Margaret Bess Clemmons

Library of Congress Control Number:		2019902965
ISBN:	Hardcover	978-1-7960-2101-1
	Softcover	978-1-7960-2102-8
	eBook	978-1-7960-2119-6

Print information available on the last page.

Rev. date: 03/15/2019

To order additional copies of this book, contact:
Xlibris
1-888-795-4274
www.Xlibris.com
Orders@Xlibris.com
793168

CONTENTS

This is the truth as I know it to be; through experiences and conversations with my mother-the finest lady I have ever known. This is our journey! It is my hope that future generations will know how blessed they are that this woman is a part of who they are.

Selah.

THE BEGINNING

In order to tell you about myself or my mother I must first tell you about the woman who raised her. I must go back deep within my memory to recall all Mom has told me. Yes, I will not remember every single detail that has been told to me through the years; however, I will try to show how extraordinary I believe the both of them to be.

My grandmother was born in the late 1800's and married young. My grandfather and she had 10 children. Grandma did the raising while Grandpa spent very little time at the homestead. My Mom had said when they first married that Grandpa had set her up in a shack in the mountains that only had a quilt hanging as a door. Grandma was with child, (pregnant was not used because that was considered disrespectful), when they had married. There were real dangers to being in that shack all alone. Rattlesnakes, copperheads, wild animals that surely any man would want to protect his wife and unborn child from let alone the harsh winter! It was rumored that Grandpa's brother was in love with her, but my grandpa had made the move first and then there would be no other since a baby would be on the way. Grandpa's brother stopped by to check on her in that shack knowing how cold it had been and I guess wondering if she was really being looked after by Grandpa. He found the quilt hanging with snow inside the doorway; there on the other side she would lay. Mom said she had probably passed out from the cold or lack of food, but it had prompted this man to threaten his brother, enough to get her out of there and build her a home in the holler of Kingdom Come. This was the only one of her in laws that had shown any kindness towards her; Mom used to think how different life might have been for her if Grandpa could have just loved her as his brother had.

My Grandma would raise her 10 children, and God only knows how many grandchildren and strays, in this home. While my grandpa would come home to help get the crops in, maybe stay long enough to produce another child, my Mom would recall him rarely being there. "Too busy cattin' around I reckon," is what she would say. She also told me many times that God walked beside her mommy as that was the only way a woman could have survived the life she lived. Mom had told me that when she was little that they still had a dirt floor that she often swept. I found this to be a silly chore and asked her why on Earth would you sweep a dirt floor? Her response, "Just because we were poor doesn't mean we had to act like we were poor Bessie! We had to take care of what we had, keep it lookin' neat and clean... you do the best with what you got!".

What they had wasn't much! My mom was born during the Great Depression not that that had made them poor, but it sure didn't help. Mom remembered being nestled in that holler not realizing just how poor they were, until you see others who are just a little better off. My grandma raised chickens, hogs, cows, and had horses for plowing. Children grow up and help out until they start 'cattin around', go to war, or die from illnesses. My Grandma lost a daughter who was just 5 years old; she had sent word to the doctor that her baby girl was sick with fever. Grandma couldn't just up and take her into town which would have meant crossing the river or swinging bridge, catching the train, and leaving all children and chores behind. Besides, the doctor was her own brother in law, another one of Grandpa's brothers. Oh, he had gotten word his little niece lay sick in bed with fever, but he had things to do. Finally, after several days and several sleepless nights for Grandma, the good doc was on his way. Grandma sent word to tell him to turn around, her baby girl had died. I am sure her heart was broken but there was no time to grieve for the work never stopped. Little lives depended on her to make it.

Mom often said how she would pray to God to keep her mommy safe; she knew that she and so many would be lost without her. She would say, "Many times Bessie I would hear my mommy go out into the dark, lantern in hand, because there was something going on in the chicken coop. Mommy couldn't afford to lose one egg or baby chick! She would go out there in the dark to who knows what and I would lay there, so little and scared that she wouldn't make it back to me! She would come through the door and I would ask what had the chickens upset; most of the time it was a black snake trying to steal eggs. My Mommy would put her hand in that nest not knowing what she would be grabbing, it could have just as easily been a copperhead and my mommy could have laid there and died!" My own mom's voice would crack telling me the story and I knew what she was feeling. Her greatest fear was losing her mommy and my greatest fear was losing mine!

Grandma heated her home with a potbellied stove fed with the coal out of the mountains. She would put on her high boots and cross the river to climb the mountain to pick the coal and fill her sack. I am sure this was a chore her boys had done when home but often it was her chore to do; she had to have it for heat and cooking. She heated water on the pit to wash clothes on a washboard and hung them to dry in the Appalachian air no matter the season. She did this for many years until finally getting a wringer washer that sat on her front porch. Mom would say you have never seen whiter whites, but scrubbing clothes was hard work. Listening, I thought it all seemed like hard work and I was glad not to be born in that time when it seemed you always worked hard, and the only way out was death itself!

Mom said, "Mommy never stopped, always work to be done. I am sure she only slept a few hours a night and then it was with one eye open. She would get awful migraines and just rub her head and go on; I never seen her lay down just to rest! I know God himself walked along side of Mommy, there is just no other way she could have withstood her life without Him!" Grandma aged fast as most people did then; their lives spent surviving not living. My grandma could have left that world behind, but she stayed. The love she had for her babies and the faith she had in God was the only things that carried her...sustained her! So many have her to thank for their own survival though I doubt she ever had much recognition.

I remember my mother's recollections of her younger days and how she helped with the chores and stayed by her mommy's side as much she could. She talked about the little joys of getting the Sears Roebuck catalog and cutting out paper dolls to play with, or cutting out beautiful flowers or backgrounds in that book to decorate the walls of her home with. Mom wouldn't even own her first real doll until she was 13. "Mommy would have loved to have given me one but there was never enough money for toys. Daddy spent his money on other people's children." I asked her about Christmas, this is what she had to say, "We always hung our socks up hoping Santy Claus would bring us something. If we were lucky, we got some nuts, an orange, and maybe a peppermint stick. I couldn't figure out why he always passed us by…we were good! Looking back, it must have hurt Mommy to know she could never give her children their wants, to see us disappointed; but really, she gave us all that we needed. I don't much care for Santy Claus- he is just a fairy tale that lets littleuns down!" My parents had always given us so much, I hurt for the little girl who would someday be my mother. I knew she deserved more then, and she deserved more now. I told her how sad it made me, that she led such a hard life without the joys that I simply took for granted. You know what she said? Well let me tell you; she said" I would live it all over again and again!". I looked at her like she had lost her mind. "Why Mom?" I asked, who would want this to be their childhood! With a faraway look and tears in her eyes she softly spoke, "Because Mommy was there!".

YOUNGUN

Growing up on Kingdom Come holler meant that most families had it hard. The kids went barefoot in the warm months and when cold set in they would get a new pair of shoes that had to last through until the next year. The shoes had to be kept in good condition, they were your school and your church shoes; money was tight so try not to scuff them or ruin them. Church was a small chapel with a cross on top where people congregated for the word and how Mom would say, "To scare the crap outta ya because you were never going to be good enough!". They spoke in tongues, shouted to the heavens to forgive all the sinners, and save those lost folk who didn't attend. You couldn't fall asleep within these walls, you were glued to the pew for fear of catching someone's attention! Mom didn't like this way of preaching the gospel; like me, she was too busy watching the antics instead of really hearing the message. She never spoke in tongues but believed those that did honestly felt the spirit and she respected that. At times there would be picnics or pie auctions afterwards, people catching up and enjoying each other's company. The auctions would be a way for the young folk to meet, she would auction her baked good and the highest bidder shared the pie with her, a date of sorts under the watchful eye of the congregation.

The schoolhouse was one room and held primmer(primary) through the eighth grade. The teacher was seen with the same respect as a parent would have been and a leather strap hung on the wall to remind you of this fact! A teacher, uncle, aunt, anyone who was your elder had the right to hand out a good whoopin' if they saw fit to do so without any repercussions from the parents… if you needed correctin' then it was going to be given to you! Mom had said one of her teachers was a man that handed out a strapping on a regular basis; she thought it to be cruel and for the most part unnecessary. She also at one time had a lady for a teacher whom she adored. She wore a grape colored lipstick and the years I spent with my mother she was always in search of the exact shade. I remember Mom buying tube after tube of shades of purple lipstick. My brothers remembered our mom wearing red, but I only remember the purple; it looked beautiful on her and to this day I look at the purple hues before any other color. Mom carried a lunch pail-not even half the size of a small coffee can- in which she carried cornbread crumbled up with milk or the occasional blackberry dumplings. This was lunch, and she was fortunate to have that as some of the smaller children would wait for their mothers to come nurse them behind the schoolhouse door! A nurse would come around every so often to give free vaccines since most could not afford to be immunized. My mom and aunt neither one wanted a shot to the arm and had concocted a plan to get out of it. After giving the injection the nurse would put a purplish mark on the site showing that the child had received their dose; Mom and my aunt had the good fortune of having blackberry pie in their pails and proceeded to mark their own arms with the drippings. It actually worked; and luckily, neither came down with a disease from the missed vaccine.

She spent the days in the field with her sister and niece who was like a sister to her since Grandma had raised her most of her life. People, mostly her own children, often let Grandma raise their children for periods of time so as to have the freedom of doing whatever they wanted without being tied down. The three grew up as sisters and best friends, sharing the hard work and joys of this time and place. They worked alongside their mommy and entertained each other in spare time. My aunt was the daredevil and my mom the scaredy cat! Mom always worried they would get caught or die from the plots her sister concocted. One time my aunt took dynamite from a mining site and decided she would blow up the mountain. Mom wanted nothing to do with this but felt compelled to go, afraid her sister whom she begged not to do something she had already set her mind to do! Off they went up into the mountain, Mom pleading the entire time for her sister not to do this. My aunt placed the dynamite, lit the fuse, ran… BOOM…success! It blew a good size hole, but it also drew the attention of their uncle who happened to be passing by on the dirt road beneath them. "What in the hell are you two doing?" My aunt replied, "Blowing up dynamite!" The uncle threatened to skin them both alive to which my aunt replied he would have to catch them first making my mom about sick knowing the trouble and whoopin' surely about to befall them. Luckily, the uncle had no time for the chase which only made my aunt feel less fear than ever. My mom admired and loved my aunt with all her heart and allowed herself to follow her even though she was terrified what she would come up with next; more terrified though of what might happen to her beloved sister if she didn't follow. My aunt knew every inch of the mountains; every plant, tree, and berry that grew within. She would tell my mom after eating a berry or plant that she would probably die; it would be up to my mom to let someone know where to find her body. Mom would cry, not even knowing how to get back home. My aunt would burst out laughing at Mom's fear; she had known all along what she was eating!

Back at home play meant running through the corn, playing hide and go seek, fishing or swimming in the river, and playing cards if one could manage to sneak a deck passed Grandma. Grandma thought cards was a devil's toy, she thought it led to drinking and gambling; men fighting over money that could have been spent feeding their children. Often Grandma would find their hidden deck of cards and without hesitation fed the potbellied stove with them. Grandma was quick with the disposal and wasted no time letting them know that there had better be no more; pleading was useless, she had seen too many times where a "friendly" card game could lead. That was that! Mom looked forward to the times when her daddy came home, she loved him and missed him as any child would. He often took her sister fishing but told Mom she couldn't go because she didn't hold her mouth right, this meant she talked too much and scared the fish. He had nicknamed her Jimmy, mom never knew why unless he had wanted another boy. She knew her daddy loved her but never understood how leaving them behind seemed so easy for him. Thankfully she had a mommy who never did! Daddy would sometimes give them a quarter to catch a movie in town and get a coke with; this was a real treat, but I think she would have rather had his time. Once her daddy had come home for a visit. He was drunk but not in a way of being playful but in a mean drunken spell. Didn't take long to realize he was there to argue with Grandma. Grandma must have said something that he took offense to because he reached into his pocket pulling out his knife. Mom heard the click of the blade and screamed, "Mommy he's got a knife!". Quicker than you could bat an eye, Grandma had him pinned to the floor of the porch and sent the knife flying into the yard. Grandpa got up and was fit to be tied but did not go back at her, he searched for his knife asking for my mom's help in finding it. After a while, he gave up and left; Mom had found the knife while he was looking and never told him. She never gave it back! He would be gone a long time, not sure if he was ashamed or scared. Had he killed her that day there would have been no one to care for the children she had seen to and there certainly would not have been any justice for a man killing his wife.

Grandma would lose a son, he was nine and he took "fits" and it was during a seizure he died. I am sure there were tears at night while everyone else slept but she didn't weep in front of her children, no time to mourn when others need you to be okay. "God walked with my Mommy, I tell you Bessie there is no other way she could have kept going!", my mom had said many times. Thank you God for walking with her, and thank you for walking with mine!

Mom was young when she watched several brothers go to fight in WWII leaving behind the hard work for little hands and her Mommy. Daddy seemed to come around a little more often to help out and to read the letters sent home by their sons. One of my Mom's brothers had received a "Dear John" letter from his sweetheart and he let anyone who read the letter know that he hoped her new beau's nuts would fall off! Mom missed this brother, Roland, the most. He was always so kind to the little ones, making time to chase them around before going into the field with Grandma doing the work of two men. He loved his mommy, and he spent most of his time trying to make her life easier instead of filling it with worry. Roland was in the Army and drove a tank. "Mommy hadn't received a letter for some time," Mom would recollect, "and then came a telegram that Roland was missing in action." They would soon find out that he was in France when the enemy had dropped a grenade into his tank; he could not officially be pronounced dead until an investigation was completed. Mom would say it must have been hard to identify who was who since that grenade wouldn't have left much to identify! Eventually he was pronounced. Grandma read that he had been buried in a nice area of France, thanking her for her son's service and offering condolences! This would be the first time Mom would see Grandma openly cry! How scary it was for her to see her strong mother weep, what if she fell apart never to become whole again? What if she no longer had the strength to take care of all who needed and depended on her? Strong women don't cry, yet she was! To know that he was dead was heart breaking; to know that his body was never coming home was devastating! He had been born and raised in the mountains and surely had wanted it to be his final resting place…being told he had been buried in a "nice plot in France" was the final slap in the face to Grandma and had allowed the flood gates to open! She would receive his purple heart pin and a small monthly allowance from his life insurance. This small monthly check allowed Grandma to keep food on the table. My own mother would say, "God works in mysterious ways. She would never had traded her son's life for that money but because of it, others lived that would have surely starved to death!".

It had been about two years after Roland's death that someone had stopped by to give Grandma a clipping from the morning newspaper which read that loved ones of those killed in action could claim their remains to be sent home for burial. Grandma petitioned for his remains and a telegraph was sent to her on the day and time to be at the train station to claim her son, not to be late because this would be a 'one time' only event and there would be no waiting! Grandma arrived two hours ahead of schedule to claim his casket – her son was home! The undertaker rumored that his casket had been empty, and I believe Grandma already knew this in her heart! However, she needed to go through the process of bringing whatever there was of him home, so she could find some kind of peace! She had brought her baby home- to the mountains of Kingdom Come- laid to rest with his siblings in the graveyard on the hill behind the church he had attended. Thanks to a mother's love her child could finally rest in peace- in spirit if not in body! This allowed Grandma to also have peace and carry on; though, a part of her own heart lay in that empty coffin!

Little would my own mother know that while all of this was going on there was another sailing on the Pacific fighting the same war as her brothers…this other man she would someday meet and would become my father!

HOME

My mother would grow into a beautiful young woman; her light sandy hair would become almost as dark as the coal dust and hung in thick, tight waves that made brushing difficult. She had a slender build, dark brown eyes, and a beautiful smile. It would have been easy for her to be whisked away by some handsome young man promising her the world but, unlike most girls, my mama wanted to stay put and be with her mommy forever. She loved being nestled in the bottomland of the mountains, the scent of pine in the air, the sunset bringing with it the sound of livestock bedding down and the crickets awakening! Mostly, she loved working beside her mommy, sister, and niece. Of course, there were suitors, but none had the appeal of sweeping her from what she loved most – being home!

There always comes a time when you must leave the place that you know to be home and there would be no exception for my mother. A friend of hers had to move to Rhode Island due to her husband being in the armed forces; she pleaded with Mom to go with her to help her settle in since she would be alone with babies of her own. The friend also pleaded with Grandma to let

Mom go. Mom went with her friend and surely must have felt guilty leaving behind her share of chores for her (now married with babies of her own) sister and the mama who was now raising several grandchildren. She went with her friend out of love for her and the need to help her. She said her goodbyes but promised to return as soon as she could. Leaving her mommy behind with tears in her eyes!

Rhode Island was nothing like the land she had left in what must have seemed like on the other side of the world. She helped her friend set up house and take care of the babies. She soon met a man who was also in the military. He took a quick liking to my mother and even fell in love with her. I assume Mom never felt quite the same way since she had never mentioned this man to me in our forty- seven years together; I only found out about him through her friend that she was living with back then. This man, I think his name was Jim, was also on detail for the military and had to leave for a brief period. Mom had met Jim at the diner that she had taken a job as a waitress. I guess she figured she could make a little money while awaiting her friend's husband to return to his family. Mom liked the diner but the people she waited on obviously had a different life than what she had known. They could afford to have a meal cooked and served to them while dressed in their best; seeming to not have a care in the world. Most of them were businessmen stopping by for a coffee on their way to the office. My mother may have been intrigued but surely not impressed. A man that could feel comfortable in a pair of dungarees while hooking up the horses to plow the field, shave the bark off the wood to saw and make planks, plant the field, nail that wood to make a floor, and still have enough time to spin a tale for his small child…now that would be impressive! Surely the customers seen my mother as adorable with her wild hair held back with a headband or clip, her southern accent, and genuine southern hospitality. They may even have assumed that this little lady from the hills of Kentucky was backwards and meek leaving her easily a pushover. One man, not a gentleman, came in one morning for his breakfast in his business suit and had summed my mother up to be just that and obviously finding her quite attractive. He was flirting with her and probably used to getting his way. As she poured his coffee, he took the liberty of touching my mother's leg with his hand…a quick, slight caress. My mother proceeded to shift the coffee pot from the cup to his lap. The man jumped from his seat scowling, yelling profanities until the diner owner came running to see what the commotion was all about! After hearing both sides of the story he told the business man in his stained trousers to leave and never return. I like to refer to this episode as, "Don't mess with a mountain woman"! They may carry themselves to be just a quaint, country girl who one may assume has no voice, but cross her and she will bite with the venom of a rattlesnake.

Eventually she would no longer have to live in Rhode Island, as her friend's husband had returned. Mom however, would never truly return home to live. She had a sister in Ohio who was the mother of her niece that had been raised with her. They were both needed there to help with the household as her sister and husband both worked. Mom would soon be in Ohio helping with her sister's family and whatever family came there looking for work. She would in all reality be a servant to those setting up a new life while her heart just wanted to go home and help her mommy. It would be at her sister's home that she would meet the mailman out at the mailbox and three months later she would marry him. This man was my father. Jim came back looking for my mom; the friend told him she had moved but did not tell him where. He wanted to ask my mom to marry him, he still loved her. The friend told him it was too late, she was already married. Thankfully for myself, things worked out the way they had, or I would not be here at this desk writing my mother's journey. My mother's plan had been never to leave the side of her mommy or the holler of Kingdom Come. Although as a child growing up, we often visited, I knew it had to be painful every time Mom said her goodbyes. Whenever she spoke of home she was referring to where her mommy was, where she had grown up poor but had all she wanted. "You can never go home again Bessie. You can visit but once you make a family you can never go back to the way things were. I loved my mommy and regret leaving her. I am happy with my life and never would I trade my kids or my husband…but I can't help to long for the days of being with Mommy, my sister, and my niece. We had nothing, but we had everything. Does that make sense?" she would say to me many times. Yes mama, I can truly say now that I get what you were saying. Home is where the heart is and like Dorothy would say, "There's no place like home!"

THE FIRST MAN I EVER LOVED

My father was a child during the Great Depression and although his family was not as poor as my mother's tough times were still had. He grew up in the times of rations, coupon books that were used when buying common goods, which meant you had to make things last. His parents had a daughter and three sons, my dad being the second youngest. I remember Dad telling me once that he had went to school without lunch. To pacify his hunger, he had added hot water to ketchup making a tomato soup if you will. Both hot water and ketchup could be obtained in the school's cafeteria and sometimes there would also be a small supply of saltines. He said it didn't happen often but when necessary he would make his "tomato soup" in order to get by.

Although his childhood had more conveniences than that of my mother's his was still no picnic! His father was a strict man who never wanted children in the first place and a kind word, praise, or even a gesture of affection from his father was not given. His mother often suffered verbal abuse and sometimes physical abuse from her husband. His mother tried to show her children affection but was often scoffed at for babying them. My Dad remained a respectful son who did anything his parents asked but his love was towards his mother. However, he did tell of a few instances where she would take him and his brother for a walk in the woods. She would lay down and act as if she were dead, sending them both into crying fits. She would soon sit up and laugh telling them she was fine, soothing them back to reality. Dad, looking back never had known why she would have done this. It seemed so cruel to him and he loved her. I think she was close to a nervous breakdown due to Grandpa's constant tirades. Grandma did love her children and fought just to carry them to term. Whenever she became pregnant Grandpa would want her to drink the herb tea his sisters had to end their own unwanted pregnancies. Grandma wouldn't which would provoke Grandpa into beating her hoping she would miscarry. None of Grandpa's sisters had children even if their husbands had longed for a child. They would drink the herb tea and if that didn't work, or was too far along, then the doctor was called to do a home visit. Basically, the doctor came and performed an at home abortion. It was one of these times, by my father's recollection, that his aunt had a late term abortion and the doctor brought out of the room a perfectly formed baby boy, already dead. The doctor proceeded to throw the infant into the grate and burned it like they would burn their trash. Dad hated his aunt from that moment on and had no respect for any of his aunts. He would refer to them as, "Tight ass bitches that love no one except themselves!". Although my dad honored his father by being respectful in their presence, he could have cared less if they had been murdered as that baby boy had been.

My dad grew up making his own happiness, mostly through pranking others. He loved his brothers and sister especially the brother that was thirteen years his junior. It was hard for my dad to show affection, so he did it in other ways; helping those when needed, giving his time, making someone laugh, buying things to make someone happy whenever he could. My uncle relayed a story how one of their aunt's and her husband had come for an overnight visit. Both wore dentures and took them out at bedtime placing them in cups on their nightstand. Dad snuck in while they slept and exchanged the cups leaving the two confused the next morning as to why their teeth no longer fit. Another time the goody two shoes of the neighborhood was having a birthday party to which Dad and his friends were not invited. Dad and the boys took a box and took turns crapping (sorry) in it. They proceeded to wrap it, placing a pretty bow on top, and left it on the girl's porch. They rang the doorbell and ran to lay low and watch. The girl and her father came to the door and saw the beautiful present. The father scooped up the gift while the girl squealed with delight, the boys stayed hidden while they laughed as well. Moments later the door swung open with the father throwing the box into the yard obviously outraged that someone had done this to his princess! Dad still laughed every time he told the story...I can still hear his laugh.

I never knew how bad things were between him and Grandpa, but I can imagine it was more than he could take at times. I know that because of his father's constant belittling that it made my Dad hardly able to give, show, or receive love even though the child inside had wanted those things. I imagine he dreamed of escape but stayed knowing shaming his father would mean harder times for his mother and siblings. WWII would provide my father's escape in an honorable way. He joined the Navy at seventeen, lying about his age to get in, but then nobody cared anyway…they needed men to fight. His older brother joined with him so that made it even more notable for my grandfather. My father left his little brother a lamb for him to take care of and love while he was away. I know it must have weighed heavy on his mind to leave but it was his chance to be free. In order to be free from the war within himself he had to join a war that would take him far from home.

My dad loved the navy life, he smiled as if dreaming every time he spoke of it. He loved the sea air, the motion of the waves, having recognition for being a hard working sailor doing all he could do for his country he loved. Dad was a man soaked with pride, intelligence, and the ability of knowing what to do and when to do it!! He loved the travel, the exploration, and especially fighting the good fight. He was there to prove himself to be a winner and he was; he always will be in my heart. These were the best days of Dad's life- he learned, excelled, and taught. He told us kids, "When I die look close at my face, you will see a smile…I had a good life!". Yes, he loved us, Mom and his kids, but I think he was smiling because of his Navy days…the days when he knew freedom.

My father officially became a member of the U.S. Navy four days after his eighteenth birthday as an apprentice seaman. He would promote to seaman 2nd class, signalman 3rd class, signalman 2nd class, signalman 1st class, and then chief quartermaster. He would take his naval training in Great Lakes, Illinois, his signal training in Chicago, and sub chaser training in Miami, Florida. He served with the U.S.S. S.C. Atlantic Fleet Patrol U.S.S. Pfeiffer D.E. 588, 7th Fleet, Philippine Sea Frontier Convoy Escort, Invasion Task Force. The war would end in 1945 and no soul had been lost on his ship during the war. However, after the official announcement of the end of war came, the celebration on ship began! They had made it! Some felt lax concerning the rules of the ship being a time of celebration. It was a strict rule on the ship never to sit on the ropes at the sides of the ship; it was during one of these celebrations that a sailor did just that. He lost his balance and fell overboard to the perilous water below. He was gone and no way to retrieve him, gone from view and gone from this life. The war was over, but his family would still be receiving a telegram or call that their loved one had perished.

My father would leave the U.S. Navy in January 1946 at the age of 21...almost serving four years and leaving with his awards which included Philippine Liberation 1 star, Asiatic Pacific 1 star, American Theater, and Good Conduct. While serving he sent money home to be put into savings, something to begin a life with. He came home to find his father had spent every cent. He had to start from scratch. He took the Ohio State Highway Patrol exam and applied to the U.S. Postal Service. He was working as a mail carrier when he found out that he had passed the exam, he chose to stay with the USPS, I am glad he did so because this is how he met my mother.

Although these writings are mostly about my mother and myself do not think for one second that I don't miss him. Dad will always be the first man I ever loved. He not only provided for our family, I seen him as bigger than life itself. He was ten feet tall in my eyes, then and now! I never knew him to lie; actually, he was quite blunt when it came to honesty. He worked harder than any man I have ever known. We needed for nothing and had everything we wanted. I knew he loved me, without words or gestures, I knew it! I could feel his love in his laughter when I was happy and in his worried look when I wasn't. I knew it in his forgiveness when I broke his heart though I never meant to. My mother would often say, "You act just like your Dad", sometimes she meant it as a compliment and sometimes she didn't, but I most certainly took it as one all of the time. I wanted to be him, I wanted to make him proud, I wanted to walk his walk…there was never a man I would ever trust more in my life…EVER!

My Dad had dreams for me, his little girl, that I would crush with a sledge hammer. The one man I never wanted to let down and promised me the world if I would only listen would find it in his heart to forgive me when I didn't. This is how I know how much he loved me! I love you too Dad, always have…..always will!

CEDAR DRIVE

My parents met while my dad was delivering mail to my aunt's house with whom my mom was staying. It was summer, and they would be married by the middle of autumn. My dad had been married briefly; as it turned out she was a bigger drinker than my dad and not much for housekeeping, so it had ended almost as soon as it began. My dad paid the last ten dollars he owed his attorney the day before he and Mom would marry. They were married at the courthouse in Kentucky with my mother's parents, her sister she had been staying with, and the sister's husband. They would spend their wedding night at The Pine Mountain Motel room 6. Their home would be made in Ohio, my mother would never live in her beloved Kentucky again.

Once married rumors started flowing through my paternal grandfather's family that my mom was pregnant and that was why Dad had married her so fast. This infuriated Dad! He made it known to Mom that they would not be starting a family for at least a year to show the gossip mongers they were wrong. Dad was absolutely the head of the household and what he said went; Mom also believed that there was a certain order of things and that the man being the head of the household meant that his wife upheld his word and decisions. My dad was the provider and Mom took care of the house. Many people said she kept the cleanest house they had ever seen! She also had supper ready for Dad when he came home from work, hot on the table. They spent most of their spare time with his parents, Dad would rarely take Mom "home" even though she was missing her parents terribly. Mom and Grandma would write to each other to stay in touch since Grandma didn't have a phone. Mom was aggravated that she rarely seen anyone on her side of the family; she thought that Dad had seen himself as better than them. I think he didn't know how to fit in or maybe he thought Mom would never want to leave.

Mom would become pregnant a couple of months after their first anniversary. Both my Grandmas would advise her on how to take care of herself. No hanging clothes on the line, this could cause the baby's cord to wrap around its neck. No watching scary shows because whatever scared you could cause your baby to be marked for life. Dad would chase Mom around the house acting like a gorilla to which his mother would scold him telling him he was going to mark the baby. My brother would be born on the hottest day of August that year. No air conditioning back then but also no pushing. Once the doctor determined you were ready to give birth, he simply had the mother breathe in gas through a mask and next thing you knew you was waking up to your baby. My brother had been born quite hairy; both grandmothers were convinced this was due to Dad acting like a gorilla!

My mother had found her true calling for she poured every ounce of her love into being the best mama ever. Our dad still rarely showed affection even though he loved them both. This would plague our family for too many years. My mom was affectionate, but Dad didn't know how to react, he often thought if she hugged him or kissed him out of the blue it must have meant she had wanted something from him or had done something that would make him mad. Mom had told me once, "I could have shown your Dad great love, but he never trusted that it was love, he always thought that I was up to something!". Eventually she tried less and gave her children the love and affection that could have been shared with my father. In so many ways Dad treated Mom more as a child than his spouse. She cooked what he wanted, and it was on the table when he wanted. She was to listen and not interrupt, keep the house spic and span, and they enjoyed the company of who he chose. She was obedient because he was the head of the household, the provider, the husband! My Grandma, who they spent much of their time with, told my mom that she was going to be old before her time. "You spend all your time with us old people," she would say, "and that is going to make you old too! You need to visit your own mother, your sisters, your people. Have friends your own age. Make my son take you to see them!". Mom wanted to do just that, but she didn't know how to approach Dad with such a request, after all, she was just his wife. My mother did not go against Dad's wishes. Once, Mom's teeth had gone bad and she had them all pulled. She had a set of dentures made but couldn't wear them just yet because of the swelling of her gums. It was Sunday which meant dinner with Dad's folks. Dad insisted she put the dentures in because she would be a sight to be seen with no teeth; she forced them onto her swollen gums as painful as it was. She sat down to dinner, but the pain was too great for her to even take a bite. Grandma noticing this asked her what was wrong, Mom just gave her a tearful look and she immediately knew! Grandma knew Mom wouldn't defy Dad and she knew it was his idea for her to wear them. Grandma abruptly stood up from the table and fetched a glass of water sitting it next to my mom's plate." Now you spit those teeth out into that glass right now and don't you put them back in until your mouth is fully healed!" She also shot a look to Dad and Grandpa that she meant exactly what she had said, and they had better keep their mouth shut! Mom pried the dentures off her swollen gums and placed them into the glass, feeling relief from the pain but also from knowing someone had taken up for her. I believe this is the day my mother truly gained another mother; she loved Grandma like her own mommy.

Finally, Dad decided to take Mom for visits to Kentucky. Guess what happened? He learned to love the place! He gained a deep respect and love for his wife's mommy and the visits became more frequent just so he could help her out with all she had to do. He was amazed by this woman and felt sorry for her as well. After my second brother was born the trips became even more frequent and by the time I arrived it was every other weekend. There were no luxuries here, it wasn't always a vacation. It was often a working weekend, but he didn't mind it. He wanted to help her have things a little easier. He worked the fields with her and carried shingles on his back across the swinging bridge to roof her house. He spent his time and money without complaint…this is how Dad showed love…he took care of things. Of course, Mom was happy to be with her mommy and worked just as hard as any man there. There were times when we brought some of our cousins back with us to give Grandma a break. Mom would enroll them in school, buy new clothes, and love them like their own mamas should have. This never seemed to bother Dad. I think he felt sorry for the kids and was glad to ease Grandma's load. Never once did I feel slighted of Mom's attention; she had all the love in the world to go around and each of her own children knew that we were always her priority. She used to say," It's probably a sin that I love my babies so much." I knew what she meant, the husband was suppose to be first and the children second, but for her it had reversed. Her children showed her affection and wanted her attention; Dad still struggled with this. Besides that, Dad was a beer drinker and every day after work he would spend a couple of hours at the bar with his buddies, so Mom spent most of her time with just us- her babies. It was something was on Dad's mind or if one of his buddies had put one of their dumbass ideas into his head, he would come home fit to be tied. This meant Mom would have to hear his hours long drunken lectures of how she wasn't raising us right, or he didn't like what she had been cooking, or whatever he deemed necessary that she wasn't doing or what she should be doing better. Mom never said a word, she cleaned the kitchen as he lectured on and on. I wonder where my mother's mind went during these episodes, she surely had left the room. Once she dared to speak back which took Dad by surprise, in retaliation he threw his plate of food on the floor and left the room. My mother cleaned it up! There is no way in hell I would have cleaned that up- the floor beneath it could have rotted and it would still have been waiting there for him. This is how I was like my dad. I was stubborn as stubborn could ever be. If I thought I was in the right there would be no changing my mind and if pushed I knew the words that would cut like a knife and leave you wishing I had punched you instead. The good things I inherited from him were his love of knowledge, problem solving- 'when there's a will there's a way', and studying people. I love to people watch as did Dad. You learn so many things watching how people interact or react without them knowing that anyone is paying attention. I had to study people because my initial instincts were so far off.

There were many times that my Dad was the life of the party. He loved joking and always had plenty of jokes and stories to tell, not everyone can tell a story and keep the audience's attention, but he sure could. He was an animal lover and was kind to children. He had a good heart. He would give you anything he had so long as you were honest with him. He earned everything he owned through hard work and had no use for liars and thieves. If us kids weren't invited then my parents didn't go, their lives had been built around us. He wasn't all bad and she wasn't all good, but I felt they were perfect for what I needed them to be; I felt blessed!

Before I was even thought of my parents purchased the lot next door to my paternal grandparents. Dad and Mom built the home I would grow up in. Cedar Drive was the name of the street we lived on, it was my heaven. But first…

My mom lay on her back painting the underbelly of the oil drum outside the house. It was mid spring and her and Dad were taking care of the outside work needing to be done at the house. As my dad passed by her, she nonchalantly let him know she was pregnant. He had said something like she was full of shit. My dad was 42 and this was something he wasn't ready to believe, he was getting too old for this. My mom was close to eleven years younger than him so it might not have been as much of a shock to her, but it definitely was for him. "I have been pregnant twice before and I know what it feels like, I am sure of it. We are having a baby!". She said it such a matter of fact way that he believed her, but it must have been hard to hear…he was 42 for crying out loud!

I was born in January weighing over nine lbs., my parents would have their first daughter and last child. My brothers were 13 and 6 and less than excited about a new baby. In fact, my oldest brother cried the day I was brought home. Maybe he had wanted a brother or maybe he didn't want a new sibling at all. Maybe he just thought I would steal his mom from him since a new baby meant more work for her and less time for him. I still don't know.

As a child on Cedar Drive, I had the best of every world. I had grandparents on one side and the best neighbors, (my second family), on the other side. Our backyard was better than any park, filled with things my dad had built for our amusement. We had huge swings, benches built around apple trees, picnic area, flower gardens, and eventually an inground pool. Dad had built a train that travelled around the yard for us and the neighbor kids to ride in. He had built me a car that went three m.p.h. that I drove on our dead end road. We had a holler for sledding, fields for my brothers to play softball in, and trails for dirt biking. Cedar Drive had the best of everything…it was magical, and I didn't even know it. Grandpa supplied me daily with a fresh bouquet out of his amazing flower gardens, and I played on the branches of my grandparents' magnolia tree- to this day magnolia is one of my favorite scents. My dad would teach me how to swim and jump off the diving board in one day. I was six and scared, but he told me not to be afraid that he would be there to catch me, he would not let me sink. I trusted his every word; so I swam, and I jumped, and I became part human and part fish! I lived in that pool more than I lived in the house. I had everything I could want and all I really needed was my family. I had it all! I wish I could go back there in that time and place, not to swim or play, not to even smell the magnolias. I would just like to be with my family and the people at the end of Cedar Drive!

LIKE MOTHER LIKE DAUGHTER

Mom would get her driver's license at the age of twenty-six. I guess she thought it time since she wanted to work. She started working at the post office with my dad, part time as a sub. Her niece, the one that was raised as her sister, was called in to work for Mom the day I was born. Mom would return to work and our neighbor became my sitter, but she was much more than that! She and her husband were mine and my brothers second set of parents, and our parents and they were the best of friends. We grew up with their children and grandchildren; the end of our street was one big family. My mom would get off work and call the neighbor to tell her to send me home. I would go flying across the yard to get home to Mama. Our routine would be making bologna sandwiches and sharing a Pepsi. We would then head to the couch for Mom to catch up on her stories, 'The Edge of Night', ' Search for Tomorrow', and 'The Guiding Light', to name a few at that time. Soon we would be tired and would take a small nap before getting back up to start that night's supper. As a little girl Mom had always said prayers with me before bedtime, 'Now I lay me down to sleep'…, she also told me I could pray anytime that God was always listening. As we lay down for our quick nap, I would say a prayer, silently, and always asking God for the same thing. One day after work we were making a run to the grocery store and I said, "I love you" to which she responded, "I love you more", back to me "I love you most", her turn 'I love you infinity". She had won, nothing topped infinity! There was no "to the moon and back" said at that time. I thought how to top her, and it dawned on me! I said "Mommy, I love you so much that when I pray, I ask God to take me first, so I will never have to live without you!". I was so proud, she could not possibly top that response but also it was the simple truth. We were still on our street when she pulled the car to the side of our one lane road and stopped the car. It must have been a warm day because I remember wearing shorts. She placed her hand on my bare knee, "Oh Bessie, it is a hard thing to lose a mommy or daddy but honey, there is no greater heartache than for a parent to lose their child. If you love me that much, then you wouldn't want me to ever feel that pain; promise me you will never pray to leave this world first…I don't know how I would ever make it losing one of my babies!". I was close to tears, my lower lip trembling. It didn't matter to me to lose the 'I love you' game, I worried about making her the promise she had asked for. If I stopped praying my prayer, then surely God would take her first and then what would happen to me? I made the promise, but I was busily scanning my brain for a new prayer that would give her what she wanted and what I needed. I finally came up with plan B, or I would think prayer B. My new improved prayer would be that we would die together, and I would never divulge it for her to ruin. I knew she would have said something like "What about your daddy and brothers, they would be so sad without us", as far as I was concerned they should be thinking ahead and coming up with their own prayer! I had to think about me and that meant I had to go with her even if that meant death for both of us...I just didn't want to ever be without her!

She taught me so many things that I will never be able to cover it all in a simple book. I could write volumes on our 47 years together. At a very young age I was afraid of the rain, no idea why. I loved swimming, taking bubble baths, and playing with the water hose but I feared the rain. One day it was pouring the rain outside, no thunder or lightening, just a steady summer shower. I saw Mom putting on her shoes and I asked where we were going. "We are going outside to play in the rain!". I did not want to go outside in the storm! "Listen, I am going to show you that there is no reason to be afraid; it isn't storming, it's just rain. Rain is a good thing. God is washing his Earth, watering the flowers and trees. God knows what He is doing Bessie; Lord knows sometimes we need the rain.". I reluctantly put on my shoes; I had a choice to face my fear with her or stay inside alone and watch from the window. No way I was staying inside so out into the downpour we went. I stepped out with my head hung so as to not let one drop touch my face. I stared at my shoes knowing that in minutes they would be soaked and reach my toes which disgusted me. I felt the rain saturate my hair causing it to stick to my back. I hated this! Mom said "Well, are you comin'?'. "No", I replied, looking up just enough to make eye contact to get my point across. I wasn't afraid because she was there, but I still hated the rain. She walked back to me and took my little hand, her skin soft with the rain; she gently nudged me to follow. Down the driveway we went, hand in hand, to the road that remained desolate most of the time since only three homes were at the end of our street. She wanted us to run up and down the street and splash through every puddle along the way. WHAT? How was I suppose to dodge the worms that were surely in those puddles if I was running? I could have let go of her hand, but she didn't leave me enough time to debate it...we were off running and hitting every puddle soaking the inside of my shoes. I found myself laughing with her as we jumped in puddles making the biggest splash we could make. Suddenly Grandma was at her kitchen door hollering at the both of us for being in the rain. "You two are going to get sick!" Mom hollered back that we would be fine. Time to go back inside found me wanting to stay outside; she had cured me of my fear and hate! I wanted to run with her through the warm rain and never release her hand from mine; I felt brave, as long as she held it. We came inside leaving our shoes inside the front door. She dried me with a towel and changed our clothes. Soon it was time for our nap and as I lay with my head on her hip, snuggled in behind her legs I started to drift off to sleep but not before prayer B.

Mom would dress me in the prettiest dresses and tied my long hair into pigtails and release me into the wonderment of our backyard. Within minutes she would be fetching my clothes as I would strip down to my underwear to play. I stayed tan in the summer, playing in the sun until I was forced to come inside because the sun had set, meaning it was time to get ready for bed. Mom slept with me for years because I was also afraid of the dark. After bathing I would climb into the crisp sheets that had hung dry in the summer air, although we had a dryer, she still hung them out in the warm months. They smelled so fresh! Mom would open the window to allow the night breeze to waft in and bring in the sandman to carry me to sleep. I snuggled close to her while listening to the cricket's song. The tree frogs would soon chime in not to be outdone. I would see the shadows on the wall provided by the moonlight and imagine those shadows to be circus animals. The sleepier I became the more the animals seemed to move across the wall as if putting on a show just for me. "Now I lay me…" she would start, and I would follow. Amen for her, prayer B for me!

Sunday mornings I awoke to the smells of her cooking breakfast. The house filled with so many scents that I lay there figuring out what we would be having. Fried eggs, biscuits and gravy, bacon or sausage…no, goetta, definitely goetta, yay my favorite! My Dad's side of the family was German meaning goetta became a staple in our home, all of us loved it and Mom prepared it perfectly! Afterwards we would go to church, dressed in our Sunday best because it was a matter of respect! However, if a person only had worn clothing then they should still be accepted into the church as Mom would point out, "You do the best you can with what you got! God wants all people of all walks in life to come, we are all his children. I don't love you less when you come in from playing just because you need a bath!" She always made time to answer my questions in a way my young mind would understand. My brothers would attend church unless they had figured a way to get out of it. Dad never went. He believed and that was enough. Mom said it was the mother's duty to lead her children to God and His word. When she didn't attend, I would go with my neighbor mom who always kept a supply of juicy fruit gum in her purse. She would give me a piece as we sat in the pew, insuring my mouth would have something to do during service. Our church was at the other end of our street, just a hair less than a mile. Our pastor and his wife sat in front of the pews in simple chairs in order to speak the words of God instead of hollering it from a pulpit. After singing a few hymns, requests taken, the younger children would head off to the backroom for our own teachings with the pastor's wife. She would help us do crafts while gently relaying the Word! They were the kindest people and I learned what they taught because the sermons were given without the antics my mother had grown up within her own church. Different strokes for different folks, my mother and I was alike in this way. Looking back, I now see how much we are alike. As a teenager I rebelled against the idea that I was like her, wanting to be more like my father. I thought her to be old fashioned and her mountain woman ways to be obsolete!

As time goes by, things we take for granted will change. The pastor and his wife would eventually retire then die and our little church, that had rarely seen even twenty people in attendance on any given Sunday, would also die. The church would be made into a house and sold. We became gypsies of sorts travelling to attend a service here or there. We really never found another home church. Instead, home became our church. Sunday mornings now meant waking up to that delicious breakfast and cleaning afterwards. I loathed this ritual, I was older now with better things to do. While cleaning like a woman on fire and requesting that I keep up, she would sing hymns and talk about the Lord. She also whistled hymns at times, oh my mom could sing and whistle better than anyone I had ever heard. To this day I can't whistle though she tried her best to teach me. One time, being the smart mouth I was and looking for every excuse to get out of work, I asked, "Didn't God himself even rest on the sabbath day?". I knew by the way she shot me that look, that she had mastered, that she was on to my game plan. "If a man's jackass falls into the ditch on the sabbath does he wait to get it out the next day? No, he gets it out of the ditch, meaning you do what needs to be done!" Yeah, I knew what it meant, back to work! She always had the answer be it through the bible or her own way of thinking. I regret now the time I spent then trying to get out of her grasp, why couldn't I see it was the best place I could have been? Youth is wasted on the young, and so is wisdom. I am sorry Mom that I was in such a hurry to grow up, I would give anything now to go back and slow it down, time moved on without me seeing it happen. Mom would say "Bessie don't be in such a hurry to grow up. Don't you know you are wishing my life away?". Forgive me Mom, that was never my intention, how I long for the days just being by your side cleaning house and listening to you sing!

FIRE AND RAIN

I have an idea of what to write before I begin a chapter. I called my best friend to tell her that I was feeling overcome with emotion as I knew this would be a hard time to reflect upon. I began to cry, and I tried to hold back. She said, "Friend, take your time and tell your story the way God leads you to. Remember this is your story and not anyone else's, your pain and loss through your eyes- you can't tell another's story, and don't spare your feelings. If you want your children and grandbabies to learn how you felt then you must show them through your eyes!". She then prayed for God above to lead me in my writings so someday when family reads this book they will learn where they came from through the heart of the writer! So, here it comes, forgive me if it causes the person reading this any pain. God thank you for my friend! God is good all the time and he gave you to me!

I lost my grandparents at a young age; actually, I never met my mom's dad- he died while she was pregnant with her second son. I knew him from my mom's stories and although, not always favorable, I could feel how much she loved him! That made me love him too! It is funny how I can love someone I never met but there are people who spend their entire lives taking care of their own child and yet not feel the bond or the love that should have come so easily. My dad's parents lived next door and I spent time with them often, running as fast as my fat legs would carry me between the neighbor's, my grandparent's, and our own home. Every child should have such a magical place to spend their childhood; I never knew why God chose me to be so blessed! On many days my younger brother and I would go to play Old Maid with Grandma. She would make us hide our eyes while she got the cards, not wanting us to get the deck without her knowledge and losing it. She would also get us a snack of milk and cookies- the kind that were shaped like windmills and had slivers of almonds in them. As we played, I always wanted to obtain the old maid which technically meant you lost at the end if left holding her. Though they both tried to tell me this I refused to listen, so I always thought myself to be the winner when actually I had lost. I think I just didn't want to listen to my brother; I defied him and drove him crazy at any cost. I defied him not only in the rules of the game but on every level I could! I tattled relentlessly, had him in trouble every chance I could get, and I was nothing short of a brat that watched his every move to take him down. I regret with all my heart that I put him through so much! My older brother was thirteen years my senior and would not have put up with my antics which made my other brother the much easier target. I love both my brothers – I regret being a thorn in their side, but it brings me to tears thinking how I treated the one! I love you both and where would I be without the two of you?

I would be five years old when my Grandma next door would have a stroke. It was April of 1972. She was in the hospital for a few days while her loved ones visited. She did not want Grandpa to visit, the years of constant bickering had left her in a loveless marriage; she knew he had had a mistress for quite some time. He kept insisting that Mom take him, but Mom always found an excuse as to why she couldn't. She was between a rock and a hard place, but she had chosen to respect Grandma's wishes. She loved her as she did her own mother and was not going to let her down. The nurse had told my mother that Grandma would be released the next day and a time to pick her up. My parents were going to have her stay with us while she got back on her feet which Grandpa didn't like. The next day Mom and our neighbor lady went to pick her up, as Mom approached her room she could see Grandma's reflection in the mirror outside the door. She was too still, and Mom knew in her heart that Grandma was dead. She hollered for a nurse who ran into the room. Yes, Grandma had passed. The nurse said she had been fine that morning and even had a visit from her husband; seems Grandpa had hired a taxi to take him to the hospital. My mom would say later she had a feeling in the pit of her very being that Grandpa had said or done something to bring her death about, " I don't know for sure, and God forgive me if I'm wrong, but that feeling has always haunted me." Before my Grandma's remains even touched the grave my Grandpa had his mistress and sister going through her things. His sisters holding up her 'granny panties' making fun of their style and size while Grandpa lit a fire and burned her belongings as well as family photos! The son that stilled lived at home, the one that had served at the same time as my dad, managed to grab a few things and give them to Mom for safe keeping. Everything else was destroyed as was any love my own father had left for his. My oldest brother knew what was going on and snuck out after dark, while the burning was going on, and let the air out of the mistress' tires- all four! Grandpa was scowling the next morning when he walked over to our house blaming the incident on someone in our home. Dad told him he knew nothing about it, which was true, and sent Grandpa on his way. Dad figured out who had let the air out, but no lecture came from it, I think he was not only amused but proud that his son had done this deed. I am sure he wished he had thought of it himself! Grandma's passing would be my first experience with death but being so young I can't recollect the details or if I was even at her funeral- I am sure I was but I was only five, so I just can't remember. My father stayed the respectful son, but he now often had spats with his father. He had loved his mother and somethings Dad just couldn't forgive.

My Grandma in Kentucky had been living with Mom's beloved sister for years as Grandma's health and mind dwindled leaving her to be a remnant of the strong woman she had been. On several occasions, during our biweekly visits, Mom pleaded to bring Mommy home with her to give my aunt a much needed break, but my aunt was reluctant. Finally, Mom wore her down and Grandma spent a few weeks with us. Mom was in seventh heaven seeing to her mama and letting me help her as much I could since I was still little. I remember Mom unwrapping her hair that was always kept neatly in a bun; it hung to the bottom of the seat in the chair she was sitting on. Long soft locks of gray, silver, and white. Mom would brush it gently before washing her and shampooing then would braid it, wrapping back into a bun that took many pins to hold. She was taken care of so lovingly, I too loved her. I would play with the smooth wrinkles on her hand, tracing the veins that showed the years of her labor. She seemed to enjoy this, maybe it soothed her tired skin. She would smile at me saying, "Ah Honey, look what happens when you get as old as me!" Mom would buy Grandma a navy blue with white polka dots dress for a family reunion, Grandma must have felt like she was queen for the day. She sat outside in a lawn chair that Dad had placed in the shade. Everyone took a turn visiting with her; everyone loved her. She would return to her daughter's home in her beloved Kentucky, she would get progressively worse until the woman I barely knew her to be all but disappeared. She would sit in her chair and as I passed she would say something like, "Those poor babies are freezing, they need a blanket on them.". There were no babies to be seen, but I had been instructed to play along since Mom and my aunt did not want her to fret needlessly. I would fetch a cover and lay it on the floor and this would appease her until the next sighting. Mom would say she was probably reliving her past, taking care of endless children, making sure they were taken care of.

My mom often told my brothers and I that we were making her 'climb the walls', this meant we were getting on her nerves and we better get busy doing something else besides driving her crazy. This was just one of those warnings she passed out, but I never knew it to be a physical possibility; I soon would! It was May,1974 when Mom got the call from my aunt that Grandma was doing much worse. She was now lying in bed in a comatose state and we needed to get there. Our parents took off work, us out of school, and Dad drove like a bat out of hell to get us there. I remember going into see Grandma lying in bed, I was looking into her eyes that were so dark I could not see any white in them. They never seemed to look back at me nor did she speak. The house was so full of family and people stopping by for a last chance to say I love you. One man, I have no idea who he was, cried that if not for her he would have died. She had taken care of him often with a meal or bed to sleep in when he had nothing. My mom did not want to leave her side, but my cousin knew that she needed a break and suggested they make a short trip into town, not to be gone long. Us kids stayed behind to play with our cousins, giving her a break from being mommy and daughter for just a brief moment. Moments before Mom's return I heard a loud wailing coming from inside the house. As the car containing my mother parked int the dirt driveway a child ran to the car and said Grandma's dead! My Mom fought to get out of the back of the car as if it were about to explode. My cousin in the front seat did the same screaming "They're a lyin', they're a lyin'" to my mama. The look on Mom's face makes me stop writing at this moment for I can't see through the tears. My mother ran past me as I stood on the porch step not knowing what to do, I had never seen my mom look this pained and it scared me into being still! After a minute or so I crept into the house where nothing could be heard but wailing. People lined the small house holding each other making it difficult to navigate, but I was on a mission to find my mommy. I rounded the corner to the hallway and there I spotted my mother literally climbing the walls! I just stood there not believing my eyes. Her arms stretched above her trying to grasp the top and her legs taking their turn to find footing. She begged God not to take her mommy and screamed, "Mommy don't leave me, don't leave without me Mommy!". Prayer B, maybe every daughter/son has one...I don't know. As she begged God to go with her mommy, I prayed that he would not take mine from me. My Dad was busy trying to bring Mom down off her climb to heaven and I was too scared to stay and watch. Neither of them knew that I was standing there watching, and I don't think I ever told them. It was painful to see and too painful for her to relive. I turned around and walked away. I walked pass the grieving back to the porch step. I would not see my parents for the rest of that day; my older cousins took care of me. I wanted my mama, but she was busy wanting hers! My Grandma's service would be back in the little church on the hill and be buried up in the graveyard behind it, alongside her husband and the children they had buried young.

The mom I had known before, the one who danced me around the kitchen and played air guitar on my armpit making me laugh, would not be seen. It was as if she had taken leave and left another in her place to care for us. She fed us, still brushed the tangles from my hair, gave hugs and kisses, repeated nightly prayer, but she was not the same. Eventually she returned but not without consequence. I really think she had had a breakdown. She now took 'nerve pills' and her hair started falling out. I don't remember how long it took but she eventually lost all her hair and had to wear a wig. She went to several doctors, but none had the answer. Sometimes she would grow back just a few white strands that she would bun with her finger and hold with one pin to place under her wig. Her hair never returned enough to go without a wig. I would see her all through her life admiring my hair which I kept long and free flowing. "Oh, what I wouldn't give to have a head full of hair. You know that the Bible says a woman's hair is her glory." Her glory had been taken from her! She wasn't a vain person, she just wanted to feel normal. She felt ugly and malformed even though those who loved her tried to reassure her that she was beautiful. We all take for granted so many things… like feeling a gentle breeze caress your hair. She would never again feel that, and it makes me sad to this very day!

My dad's father would die when I was eleven. He had married his mistress and moved from Cedar Drive. He became ill with cancer, my parents brought him to our home to take care of him. I remember him talking out of his head in pain. He would be talking to people from his past. I was sad when he died, his was a miserable death.

Time flew by even though it seemed to me to be dragging, I couldn't wait to be a teenager. I couldn't wait to start driving. I couldn't wait for this or that, all the while hearing Mom, "Don't you know Bessie you are wishing my life away?". No, I didn't know that, I was growing up, but I neglected to realize that she was getting older as I grew. I never saw her aging, but it was happening without my recognition. My brothers had married and was producing grandchildren, and this brought about a miracle of sorts. My parents loved being grandpa and grandma but the change that took place in my dad was unbelievable. The man I knew who had great difficulty with affection was now hugging and kissing grandbabies all the time. He would thwart every decision their parents had made and side with babies every time. If they wanted to go swimming and Mommy and Daddy said no it was Grandpa to the rescue. "Why in the hell did I put a pool in if you aren't going to let them get in it?",he would ask. "Go ahead kids, get in the pool. You can go in your underwear! Gee whiz, I tell you, I can't figure you all out sometimes. Letting them stand there at the fence looking to get in!" What could be said, he was still head of the family and no one was going to take him on in an argument so, there they went jumping into the pool, smiling all the way because they had their grandpa wrapped around their little fingers! They would win every single time! While the parents seethed, Dad would stand watch at the pool. He would be dripping with sweat from the yardwork he had been doing prior to arguing his grandbabies' case. He loved watching them, laughing out loud and calling to Mom, "Did you see that Grandma, she swims like a fish!" He raised a garden and planted strawberries for his babies to pick. He had a small section of grapevines so they could walk through and pick grapes. When the oldest was born, he built a stagecoach that was pulled by the mower. I would get in and sit the lil one on my lap while Dad drove us around the yard. The man I knew had very little time for play as a dad. The grandpa he became had all the time in the world to play! He took the grandson for a train ride and bought him a battery powered car to ride around the yard. He bought the girls their first big girl bikes. He teased and joked with them over anything he could think of. He became the man he had wanted to be and spent so many years trying to find. He was all about the fun and was so carefree with them.

My oldest brother and his wife produced children like rabbits it seemed. His wife who I will now refer to as my sister-because that is what she is-was first pregnant very young. She would suffer a miscarriage due to a tubular pregnancy. They soon had a daughter then another. She was pregnant again and was working with my parents at the post office. She had taken a fall and days later would end up at the hospital in pain. The doctor said the placenta was pulling away from the uterine wall and he needed to perform an emergency c section. I went to the hospital with a friend and some other family members and waited for the news of the birth of the premature baby. I prayed but wasn't worried; I knew things would be okay. I saw my brother's face as he rounded the corner where we had been waiting. It was a look of deep despair. He looked at us and dropped to his knees crying. I ran to him; the baby had been stillborn. I remembered Mom saying that losing a child was the worst thing a parent could have happen to them, by the look on his face it had to be true! He hugged me saying "Help me." There was nothing I could do but hold him. My sister was going to be okay, but she was still under sedation, so she would not know until she awoke. They had come to the hospital scared but expecting to leave with their baby girl, named after Mom's mother, but when they would leave there would be no baby to carry, just a daughter to bury. Back at the house Dad stood at the kitchen sink while my Mom stood at the stove with her back to us, probably cleaning it because that is what she did when upset. I stood there silently, not knowing what to do or say, just waiting to listen for words that would make sense of this tragedy. I have always been like my dad in the sense of being uncomfortable when it comes to comforting another. It isn't that we don't feel, we actually feel too much. We are both deep thinkers and it is the hardest thing to reach out when your grief is choking you. The best thing you can do is listen to another person spill their thoughts and tears but neither one of us had the ability to really reach out and take on the pain of another. It sounds selfish I know, but it isn't. We were fixers, and this was out of our ability to fix, so we stay strong to do what we can do, we remain your rock to lean on. If we take in your grief on top of our own, we will crumble; then there will be no rock to hold you steady. I watched my dad closely waiting to show me how to remain the rock. He spoke to my mother, "Why would God take a child that this family wanted and loved and give others children whose parents will give them a life of misery?". Then my dad did something I had never seen him do...he cried. It was the first and last time I had witnessed my father crying. He choked on inaudible words! My mother spun around from the stove, "Man, you got to have faith!" taking his hand into hers. "We are not suppose to question why, I know it is hard, but the Lord knows what he is doing! None of us wanted to lose this baby but we do know she is in the arms of Jesus!". Faith can carry us through our darkest hour, or it can vanish. It can make you thank Him that there's a heaven- a chance to be reunited. The loss of it can make you curse His holy name in anger trying to understand His plan. My dad was somewhere in between, looking for which side to choose. My mother would help him find it, just as she had taught him to love!

When I was born my mom named me after her sister and my middle name was my grandma's nickname as a child. Mom had been talking with my uncle, it had been brought up that as a little girl my grandma had been called Bess. My uncle said, "Bess? Why I wouldn't name a dog that!". My mother took this as a shot against her mommy and she knew right then and there that would be my middle name and the name I would go by. I am sure my uncle was teasing, but no one made jokes at her mommy's expense! Dad would always jokingly call me 'Bessie beebee full of peepee", probably because as a youngun I would pee on the driveway not wanting to waste time coming into the house! I was the apple of my dad's eye and I knew it. I would soon crush his dreams for me. He bought me my first car, hidden in the neighbor's garage for me to find on my sixteenth birthday! Dad always gave the real surprise gifts whereas Mom was practical. Again and again Dad gave to me, Mom too, for me to repay them with a broken heart. I had several boyfriends through my teen years, at seventeen I became engaged. My dad wasn't too happy, but Mom allowed it thinking I might be 'getting those thoughts that young girls do', oh mama if you only knew. I had acted on those thoughts way before now. I was looking forward to my upcoming nuptials still months away when I discovered something wasn't normal. I had missed my period and scared to death I purchased a home pregnancy test. My parents were at work and the only one home was the wife of my brother (the one who was six years older than me) and I told her what I was about to do; I swore her to secrecy! I peed on the stick and waited. I looked at the stick after waiting the allotted time and could not believe my eyes. I walked out of the bathroom down the steps and there was my sister in law waiting. She said,"Well?", and I told her- I was pregnant! She then asked how I felt about it.

"Scared." I said. In a couple of days I had Friend go with me to the doctor to have it confirmed. Yep, going to have a baby. "What do you want to do about this?" he asked. I knew he was asking if I wanted an abortion. "I'm having a baby, that is what I am going to do!" Enough said, as I walked out, I made my next appointment for prenatal care.

My soon to be husband thought it to be cool, but I was scared to tell my parents. I knew they would want me to keep my baby, I just didn't want to let them down. I didn't want them to know I wasn't who they thought me to be. However, I knew I could not keep it a secret for even a day, I would be a nervous wreck, so I decided I would tell Mom that evening after work while Dad would be out with his buddies. I made the father of our child be there while I told her. He reluctantly obliged. My Mom was sitting in the recliner watching a program on the television, we sat down next to her on the couch. I was the one sitting closest to her which allowed him the good fortune of hiding his face behind my shoulder, obviously letting me basically handle this alone. I said, "Mom, what is the worst thing I could tell you?", I stumbled for the right way to break it to her and that is what I came up with, unbelievable. She never even turned away from her show and said, "I guess if you said you were pregnant", she said it knowing that it wasn't what she was going to hear. I said, "I am". Her head spun to look at me hoping to see that I was joking. I wasn't. She kept saying with a cracking her voice, "Oh Bess, Bessie. Why? Why?". There, I said the words that she had assumed I wouldn't be saying for years to come, but I said them, and she had heard them. She stood up and left the house, walking down Cedar Drive. She would return a short while later and said that I was not to tell Dad, she would. She told my boyfriend to go home and for me to go to bed. I am sure she cried her heart out before Dad came home. She told him the next day at work, I'm guessing so he would keep his composure. That evening I came home to find Mom cleaning the kitchen and Dad sitting at the table. He had skipped meeting up with his buddies to be home when I came in. Oh God I thought, he knows! My mother said,"Have a seat, your dad wants to talk to you." He sat at the head of the table while I chose the seat to his left leaving an open chair in between us in case Mom would want to sit down and save me. She didn't, but stayed in the kitchen to listen. I can't recall all he said but none of it was good. I hung my head while he told me now I would have to marry even though he had hoped I would change my mind. He proceeded to tell me that the wedding dress I had just bought wasn't going to fit two months from now. Why I felt to open my mouth is beyond me, but I did. I said, "I bought it one size bigger." He shot a look at me that let me read his mind. "I bought the one I liked, I wasn't planning to get pregnant, that's the only size they had left, I knew I could have it altered.". Stupid, stupid, stupid! Why had I opened my mouth! I saw the hurt in his eyes, he didn't cry but I know he wanted to. The lecture he gave seemed like hours long, in the end he got up and went to bed. My mom peeked at me from the kitchen counter, "You okay?." I said "Yeah", knowing my mom would forgive but not Dad. " Okay then, go to bed. I'll see you in the morning."

The wedding took place as planned and I wore the dress that now needed no altering. My dad gave me away in the gazebo he had built for the occasion in our backyard. He gave away the daughter he dreamed would become a nurse, marry a doctor, use her intelligence to do great things! He let her walk down that grassy path to let her go…his hopes for her trailing off into the wind like the pedals she walked on. Yes, he still loved me, but he was no longer proud of me. I tarnished his good name, I had shamed him. That was the truth. My daughter would be born a little over five months later, a beautiful bundle of love in my arms. I was different, I now was a mommy. We had planned to stay with Mom and Dad the first couple of weeks after her birth, just in case I needed help adjusting. The doctor had given us a clean bill of health and had set to release us the next morning. I wanted to go home, I wanted to show her to Dad. The doctor allowed us to go home that night. We pulled quietly into my parent's driveway so as to surprise them. My husband wanted to carry our newborn into the house, but I wouldn't allow it. I had to be the one to show her to Dad, I had to connect back to him and this might be the only way. We walked in and Mom was so happy, making over her newest grandbaby. I followed her up the steps to the bedroom where Dad was sleeping. She called his name and told him there was a surprise here for him and to sit up. I walked in as he sat up in bed, I placed her in his arms. He immediately smiled and held her at arm's length to check her out. "Gee whiz, will you look at this Grandma. Look how alert she is, she acts like she is trying to coo already!". I watched his face, he loved her instantly. This beautiful baby came from his daughter. I saw new dreams awaken in his eyes. I saw forgiveness when he looked into mine! Thank you God! Twenty months later I would have another daughter who took to my dad like bears to honey. She would crawl upon his lap to suck her finger and fall asleep. It tickled Dad that she took it upon herself to make him her nap spot without even asking. He loved the attention his grandkids poured on him and I loved seeing Dad change into the man that he always wanted to be. He accepted their love and gave them his so freely- a beautiful sight to behold. Mom, of course, had always been a natural grandma. The two of them together were the perfect grandparents...just ask any of those babies...they will be sure to tell you so!

Mom was the best mother a kid could have but as a grandma she shined. She was the one they begged for sleepovers, trips to Walmart, breakfast at Mc Donald's, and who lined them up on her bed to be fed sugar loaded cheerios. She gave into their every whim! She would sing them folk songs as she had her own children and taught them about Mommy! She taught them to respect their parents although she was often the ' go between' person. If you got out of hand she would chase you down with the broom to give you a quick swat on the butt. When really tested she would grab the pinky finger, fold it and squeeze. This was called 'milk your mouse' and we would drop to our knees as soon as she reached that pinky finger. Her children and grandchildren had all experienced the pain of 'milk your mouse' as we got older.

Little ones didn't get this punishment because they were too little and that would be cruel, but if the bigger kids felt froggy then you were going to get it. Each time the one who had pushed her to far would fall to their knees begging her 'No'. She didn't even have to squeeze, just the thought was enough. While holding your pinky she would ask, "You gonna do that again, you want me to squeeze it? Next time I will Honey, don't think I won't!".

You had to laugh when she let go, she was crazy funny pulling her mountain woman tactics. She was also the one they ran to for comfort, she gave the best hugs! She consumed their love just as she had her own children's. She fed them down home cookin'… fried apple pies, gingerbread stack cake, warm pudding, the best fudge, potato salad, corn bread and milk, and every delightful thing you would want. Sundays the entire family gathered for her breakfast. She bounced babies on her knees and smothered each one with kisses. She teared up saying again, "It has to be a sin to love these babies so much!". No mama, it's a sin so many don't.

1969, when I was just two years old, Dad would have his first heart attack. He loved his beer and non filtered camels. He ate what he wanted which consisted of some pretty weird stuff I thought- fresh ground, raw hamburger with a thick slice of bermuda onion and lindberger cheese stuffed in between dark rye bread. His heart problems lead to multiple surgeries including bypasses to quadruple bypasses. As he aged, he would tone it down to less and less beer especially after he retired. He changed to filtered cigarettes and later to a pipe containing the best smelling cherry tobacco. He still ate whatever he wanted and didn't worry about exercise since the man never stopped wearing himself out with projects and upkeep. Dad had grayed but I never seen him as old. In his late sixties he still outdid any man I knew in their twenties. 1993 Dad would have his last heart attack. It was a Wednesday evening and he had sat down in his recliner to watch 'Home Improvement', his favorite show. He had taken some salami and crackers with him. Mom received a call from a friend who had a union question. Dad had once been the steward at the post office where I now worked along with Mom and the friend. She hollered his name to come to the phone, she could see from where she was standing upstairs that he didn't move. Mom knew…she screamed his name and her friend called the squad. Dad was gone in his comfy chair, watching his favorite show, in the home he had built for his family and raised them in. I guess he went the way he had wanted to go, at peace in his home with his sweetheart upstairs in the kitchen where they had shared the one and only dance in their marriage. As he held her close and danced her around the floor, he pressed his face to hers. He sang her 'Always' into her ear for only her to hear. A memory she cherished. She had lost her husband, we had lost our dad, but the memory of hearing 'I will love you always' would never be lost and the dance not forgotten.

I had been to my parent's house on the Monday prior, picking up my girls after I got off from work. As we were leaving, I told them to give their Grandpa a hug and kiss goodbye. While I watched my dad lean into to receive his hugs and kisses, I remember thinking- I should give him a hug and kiss…oh well, I will next time. I was in a hurry to get home, there was homework, baths, and just so much to do! The girls wanted to go back the next day so as I left, I told Mom and Dad I would see them tomorrow. Tuesday, I received my tax refund in the mail and cancelled with my parents, I wanted to go shopping with my girls. The girls were upset but we did what I wanted, shopping. We would go over on the weekend! I got the call late Wednesday night, after 9p.m., my Mom's friend that had been on the phone with her called to tell me she had called the squad for Dad and I needed to get over to the house. My sitter came to stay with my girls. I drove as fast as

I could. I passed the squad on Cedar Drive going slowly with no sirens blaring. I knew my Dad was in that squad, but I had to get Mom, she would need a ride to the hospital. I walked through the front door finding my mother sitting on the steps crying. I believe both my brothers were already there. I asked frantically, "What is going on? Is Dad going to be okay?" Mom looked up enough to say, " He's gone Bessie. Your daddy died." My head could have burst! I was screaming inside my head "Oh God, Oh God No." They had not pronounced him dead, so I was hoping there was a mistake, I needed to go to the hospital,…"Hang on Dad I'm on my way!". We all went and as soon as we entered, they took us to a private room to let the pastor talk to us, confirming what our hearts knew but the mind did not hear. I said, "I want to see him!". I was being assured we would each get our chance but I felt panicked…"I want to see him now!" My brother walked in with me and lay his head next to Dad's arm and cried. I looked into his face, his eyes were closed, his ears purple on the top, no rise and fall of his chest! It was true! How can this be? I thought about the inkling I had on Monday – the kiss goodbye I had promised to give the next time I would see him. I bent over him and kissed his cheek knowing I would not receive it back, knowing he would not feel it. Did he even know how much I loved him? Everyone has regrets, it would be the biggest regret I carry to this day that I didn't listen to my inner self on that previous Monday night. God had put the thought there in my head and the devil himself walked me out the door! I spent the rest of my tax refund on the opening and closing of his grave. The money I spent I would have gladly given under any circumstance, but the real truth is it came from guilt, and guilt can be as powerful as love.

I have spent a lifetime it seems with my demons- I call them Guilt and Regret. I thought I had learned my lesson from them and never associate with them again...I was wrong, so very wrong! They would show up again in the summer of 2002, reminding me that I never learn!

I remember thinking that morning while delivering my mail route that it was such a beautiful morning. Even though it was August, it wasn't hot, it was a perfect 83 degrees and low humidity. How could I have known that this day was going to be the most horrible day ever in spite of the sun shining? I could write a whole book on just this tragedy; however, I wouldn't be able to give in justice. I will reflect, but not tell the entire story about this day, I feel it isn't my place. That day my brother and sister lost another child, their seventeen year old daughter in a car crash. She died along with her boyfriend and two of their friends. This devastated our family, especially her parents and sisters. We met at the hospital praying that she would be okay; she hadn't even made it there! As my mom and I heard the worst words that would rip through our hearts from the nurse I see my mom's knees go weak. I couldn't watch and turned away as the nurse grabbed her. Yes, I feel awful, but remember, I can't comfort another when grief takes over. I was in someone else's body, this can't be happening. One detail after another pushed me further away from my body. My mother was facing her worst fear, my brother and sister was facing theirs... again! The three remaining sisters was trying to hold each other up and make sense that their journey with their sister had ended. I cannot begin to tell you how they felt except for what I saw… unbelievable pain! There was grief for our loss but also the loss of three other children and their families. Once again came my unwanted companions, guilt and regret, they always showed up when I least wanted them to. I love my niece and I have missed her greatly ever since the moment I had been told she was gone, but guilt and regret reminded me that I had been mad at her for taunting my daughter. I could have been the adult and talked to her but instead chose to be mad, besides something would come along to pull us back together… something came along, just not what I could have ever imagined or wanted. I poured myself into trying to be there for my brother's family but of course, no effort or deed can replace a beloved child. It would pull our family together… for a time! I was able to comfort the best I could, and I cried with Mom as we grieved our loss. My youngest had dated the passenger who grabbed the wheel and caused the car to spin out of the driver's control. There would be rumors, funerals, court dates, witnesses…. So much to listen to and endure. Each one of us changed just trying to find a way to live without her. Nothing would ever be the same. Our best days in life had already been lived and a gaping hole was left that could never be filled. My youngest joined the service, she said she couldn't stand being where everything was a reminder of good or bad times, even the good memories were painful now. She was there a short while and was discharged . She learned while away that it doesn't matter how far you go, grief will follow. Years later she would be back in a relationship with the young man who had caused the crash and our family was torn apart. I understand this, I really do! I also knew it wouldn't last. I know my daughter better than anyone, and I knew why she chanced losing everyone to be with him. It wasn't about love, even though she tried to trick herself into thinking it, it was about being with the last person to have been with her cousin. She wanted to know her last thoughts, her last words, her final moments... she wanted to know why, what really happened... the truth. He was looking for redemption, forgiveness from one person. Neither found what they were looking for and it ended like I knew it would. It is hard to watch your child making a huge mistake and waiting for that child to learn from it. It is even harder to know some would never forgive her even though she loved her too! She was wrong but not unforgiveable. She still cries to be forgiven, feeling ignored and exiled. No one can hurt her or punish her more than she already has herself. Her skeleton was out of the closet for the world – her family- to see. Who reading this doesn't have a skeleton that would be devastating to them if revealed? I know I do! I wanted to be the glue that held us together, just like Mom always had, but I have failed. I failed my family and I failed my daughter. I pray love finds a way, it will never be the same, but family is important enough to try. We all loved our girl who now lives in heaven with her siblings, her grandparents, her boyfriend, and friends. Never let guilt and regret become your companions as they have power they don't deserve. I had to find a way to forgive the driver and passenger although I never want them to be in my life any more than they have already been. They are not my family, but I hope their lives have learned from their tragic mistakes made on what started out as a beautiful August day. I hope our family will do the same before ' somethin comes along to pull us back together'.

A couple of years ago I was sitting in the grocery store's parking lot shutting the vehicle off to go in and pick up a few things then head home. Memories of Mom kept trying to distract me all day and I had fought them off. I didn't want to be sad; frankly, I was tired of it. I just wanted one day without thought, one freaking day! As I started out the door of my truck it came a downpour of rain, I sat back in the seat deciding to wait it out. I waited, the rain picked up. Seriously? I started thinking about the puddle jumping…no not today! I turned on the radio and realized I had the cd in from her funeral, the music we all had picked as a family. I shut it off, still raining! I remember her taking my hand and I started to cry…Why God Why…just let me be! The memory pushed its way through my wall I was trying to build, I could feel it turning to dust and pebbles with each tear that fell. Okay, you win…I would cry harder than I had in quite a while. No one dashing through the lot could hear my sobs as the rain continued and I was not seen as it was now past dusk. It rained while I remembered, maybe the heavens were crying with me, maybe it was Mom wanting to remind me that she still held my hand. I exhausted myself to the point I had no tears left to give. The rain stopped, and I could hear her say "Lord knows we need the rain!". I did need that rain; she wanted to spend time with me, and the rain made me still and give us that! The rain is cleansing, it washes and renews, everything becomes a little greener after. Fire can do the same, it strips away the old to make room for the new. The forest destroyed by fire will rest and then become alive again with brand new foliage; the trick is to get past the destruction so healing can begin. You won't be the same, but you can still be renewed. You can be better than before and still live with the scarring of the fire. Just let the rain fall and cleanse your soul, don't let it drown the person you were meant to be...the person made in His image.

THE HOURGLASS

Everyone has this hourglass with the sands of time passing through it. Some have few grains; some have many. Mom used to say that God gives us a gift of never knowing the exact moment of when our last breath will be taken. "The person laying close to death may know they don't have long to live but they don't know the exact moment. If they did they would worry so much that they might miss something God wouldn't want them to miss. It is a gift, just like free will, God gives you free will and you decide the life you will live. Hopefully, you choose wisely, we are all sinners and guilty of bad choices. We can be forgiven, just believe in him Bessie, never make the mistake of denying his existence. If someone threatens your life because you believe, then let them take your life! Be afraid of the one who can take your soul...never deny that He is Lord!" My mom gave me many sermons and sometimes she scared me to the point I had to argue my side to feel like I wasn't going to hell. I feared the end of time, I wouldn't make it I thought to myself. She seen my fear and knew I argued because of it. "All you have to do is believe! Have faith, God will take his children out, so many will be saved in the end...the faithful don't dread it, they look forward to it!". She thought as I grew that I was her rock, little did she know she was mine!

I remember the hymns she sung, "How great thou art", she sang so beautifully. She could hit high and low notes, I tried to keep up with her. She would also sing me folk songs as a child. 'Pretty Polly' being my favorite – I thought it delightfully scary. I would later in life hear her sing to her grandbabies, they loved it as much as I had. She had a way about her that was so gentle, her lullabies and back scratches always seemed to put the babies to sleep, or she would gently rub their arm taking all their concerns away. It was good to be loved by her and every one of her babies wanted her attention which sometimes caused rivalry. She loved equally, some thought she had favorites, she didn't. She understood the ones without both parents might need a little extra, she knew how it felt to long for a missing parent. That being said, she did love them all with her entire heart. None of us could ever say that she wasn't there for us. Sometimes she was our shoulder to cry on or our biggest fan, she was our moral compass and loved us no less when we failed! She fed us when we were hungry and gave us the last cent she had to make our lives easier. Where would we be without her... where are we now?

I have seen Mom help my brother paint his car, I have seen her help Dad fix things around the house, I have seen her make fudge at someone's request even though she was worn out from working her route that day. She never said 'no', she gave us all she had so we might be happy. I look around and see no other like her. Sometimes, in the mirror, I think I catch a glimpse but the woman looking back only wishes to be her.

Mom loved to mow grass and paint walls, our house must have had 20 plus coats on each wall. "It is the cheapest way to redecorate", she would say. My sister would say that she hoped heaven had walls to paint and grass to mow! We have all seen Mom get on the roof to sweep because it needed it. She was bound and determined to take care of what she had and had married a man who thought the same way. They were a team that could not be outworked, that's for sure!

Mom was full of southern sayings and home remedies, much to my amusement. I wish now I had written down those remedies because they actually worked. "Berries are the best thing goin'. You feed 'em to the babies when they can't poop, when they have the runs you cook the berry and give them the juice." Her berry of choice was the blackberry, which to my dismay meant blackberry pickin'- another chore if she was able to find a patch. Doing any chore with her was never boring; I just always wanted to be doing something else. I look back and wonder why I squandered so much time I could have had with her. I just thought she would always be; I thought there would always be more time. The hourglass never stops letting the sand sift through, I wish now I had realized this. I thought her hour glass to be as full as mine, but no one can know, the glass sits in a place not in our sight.

She spent her life with us making sure we were loved and making us feel as if we had great worth. Did I give enough back? I sat and listened to her stories of home; sometimes laughing, sometimes crying. Her world was far different from mine. So much injustice she would tell of that I would be in a rage. "I don't tell you to upset you, I tell you because I have to tell someone.

I didn't mean to burden you!" She wasn't burdening me, I just wanted to take the pain away; all I could do was listen.

Many of these stories I can't write about, she wouldn't want it in print. Stories of abuse of all kinds. It is evident to me that a child's life and that of a woman's was not respected like a man's was during her days. One story I can share is that of her aunt. She was married to an abusive husband. One day, while she was working in her vegetable garden, her husband was walking towards her- she could see by his facial expression that he was coming to beat her. There was an axe stuck in a stump closer to her than him, she grabbed it and struck him. She had split his head open, it took him three days to die. Before dying he had told the people that visited that he was in fact going to beat her and she had acted in self defense; he pleaded that she not be held accountable for his death. He died, and she was arrested; she served nine years in prison. When she did get out she would eventually remarry. Her brother came to see her one day and to help her in the garden. She offered him one of her husband's beers. My grandpa and her husband returned to hear her story that her brother had stolen one of his beers, the man went out into the field and killed him... over a beer! She had lied and her brother, a good man by Mom's account, lay dead. To cover up the murder they lay his body on the railroad tracks and let the train coming through the night run over him. Everyone thought this is how he died, my grandpa new better. I can understand the fear she may have had since she had been abused and served time, but she had set her own brother up and he paid with his life. There wasn't much of a justice system, especially if you were a woman. If a child was abused it was overlooked, people didn't interfere with another man's family. If a man raped a child, it was often the child that was punished. I was infuriated, wanting to travel back in time and hand out punishment! "Vengeance is mine sayeth the Lord.", she would say. I never had the patience of Job; actually, I had no patience at all then. Maybe I just couldn't take not being able to fix what she had seen in her life, it killed me to be so helpless. To sit and listen, my blood would boil, I listened only because she needed me to! If she hadn't had such a saint of a mommy life would have made her bitter; instead she gave it to God to sort out and me to listen.

We were cleaning house one morning, deep cleaning, so it must have been a Sunday. I was about fourteen I guess. She had handed me the piano stool that sat at her electric organ and told me to take it downstairs. Instead, I took the stool and started practicing a trick that I had seen my brothers trying to master. The trick was to place a chair between yourself and a wall, then bend so that the top of your head is touching the wall. Once in place you have to pick up the chair and then straighten up to a standing position. The hard part is standing up after you have picked up the chair, most of the time impossible to do. After a couple of times of trying I had mastered it, I could pick up the chair, remove my head from its position on the wall and stand straight up. I must have repeated it a dozen times before I heard Mom in frustration say, "Ponmysasswordohonor if you don't get movin' with that chair….", I looked at her with a smirk on my face and asked, "What in the heck did you just say?". She gave her answer in the form of a slap across my face. Now I have had a spanking, but I don't ever remember a slap across my face with such force. It wasn't going to leave a mark, but it definitely stung! I looked at her in total shock while touching my face. What had I done to warrant this? She eyed me, and I could see the hurt in her eyes, then she said something that would floor me. "Don't you ever make fun of my mommy... I won't put up with that!" Never would I have ever thought of making fun of the woman who I considered to be closer to God than anyone I had ever known including my own mother. Through vague memories and stories told by Mom, I had loved my grandma with all my heart, for Mom to think I would in any way degrade Grandma truly hurt me. I asked, "Mom, I honestly didn't know what you had said, I didn't understand what you were saying. I would never make fun of Grandma. Why do you think that?" My mom turned to me, sniffling as she spoke, "Mommy used to say 'upon my last word of honor' which means the same as 'I swear'. My mommy didn't swear so she would say this phrase instead, sometimes saying it so fast it sounded like one long word, I thought you had heard me say this before and knew it was from my mommy. I can't take anyone making fun of her! I'm sorry Bessie, I thought you were making fun. I shouldn't have hit you.". I looked at her and was sad that she thought I would ever intentionally hurt her through the love she had for her mommy. "Mom, I would never have one bad thing to say about Grandma nor would I have reason to poke fun at her! I love her too, because of you I know what a wonderful person she was. I will always respect and love her; more than that, I would never do anything to hurt you so much. Don't be sorry for the slap, I was being a brat anyway, just know I love her and you too much to ever ridicule Grandma!"

That day has always haunted me a little; not because of the slap but I think I realized just how much Mom missed her mommy. I always seen tears in her eyes when she spoke of her, but she was still ready to fight to protect her. Her love for her mama never faded with time, it may have even become stronger. She clung to the memories, the stories, to keep her love alive and fresh. She would do this until her last grain of sand fell through the hourglass!

CHANGE OF SEASON

Mom had had her share of illnesses and surgeries. She had a hysterectomy due to endometrium cancer. She had an aneurysm in her abdomen that had to be fixed. She continued on the antidepressants for the rest of her life. Menopause made her into a woman I rarely knew, making her so moody and she tired easily.

She kept up with her social engagements…bowling, cookouts, and visiting with friends. The trips to Kentucky became fewer and far between after the passing of Grandma and, later on, Dad. Soon life became about keeping up with the grandkids and the mowing of the lawn. If there was a kid sick at school, she went and picked them up. If one of her children's grass needed mowing, we would come home to find her cutting it. Whatever anyone needed she was there lending a hand and ordering Angilo's pizza to feed us all. If we were sick, she picked up our prescriptions and called you every night to make sure you had taken them. I remember having surgery and contracting E.coli, I almost died but it was her praying on her knees at my bedside that saved me… I even told my doctor this before firing him. She gave more than any of us ever gave back.

I came into the kitchen after work, she told me the doctor had called about some tests she had done. He told her she had a sizeable aneurysm in her aorta, not taken care of it would burst and she would die before ever reaching the phone to call for help. Fixing it would mean a surgery that many had rejected due to the high risk and quite lengthy and difficult recuperation. She had to go see a vascular surgeon and her doctor was setting up an appointment. About that time one of my brothers had come into the kitchen and she started to tell him what she had just told me. He looked at me to see what I was thinking; I busted out crying. This freaked him out, he knew it was serious. I blurted out every little detail that she had just sprung on me except I was not calm one bit. Mom was like, "Now you two, there ain't no need to worry. I'll be fine and if not then you have to accept that it is God's will. He is always good, and He knows what he is doing." She always said things that you couldn't argue with for fear of making God upset with you. In a couple of days she received the call of a confirmed appointment. I took her to see the vascular surgeon who spoke to us in great detail; she would have to have the surgery to have any chance at all, she was a ticking time bomb. He didn't sugar coat it for us though Mom had little reaction. I asked all the questions and he even drew a sketch for me to understand it better. It would be a lengthy surgery and no guarantees that she would survive it. He would have to graft her aorta from the previous site in her abdomen up to the base of her neck. She would spend weeks in the hospital and then to a rehabilitation center. He would have to remove spinal fluid and shut down her kidneys. Her recovery would be at least a year. He motioned towards his window that gave a view of Interstate 75. He said this surgery will be like her standing out there and being hit by a Mack truck; without the surgery she would eventually rupture and drop where she had stood. Mom said she would do the surgery; I knew it had to be done; I was scared to death as she seemed unphased. "Well you know me Honey, I'm too stupid to understand half of what he said…that's why I let you do all the talking.". Mom wasn't stupid, she often said it thinking I was so much smarter, she just hadn't listened. She didn't want to know!

Days before her scheduled surgery I sat down at her kitchen table. I wanted to talk, not leave things unspoken that I would regret later if worse came to worst. She came down the hallway from her bedroom, her shoes clicking on the hardwood floor. I hadn't knocked, none of us ever did, so she didn't know at first that I was sitting there…waiting and thinking! She wore a red sweater and blue slacks, and I could smell the recently sprayed scent of her Secret deodorant. She looked up and said, "Well, there's my girl. How's my Bessie today? Is somethin' wrong honey?". "No Mom, I just came to talk, you gotta minute?", I asked. "Sure, what's on your mind my lady?". I loved for her to call me that, I belonged to her and it made me special. She said it to others too but it was just her and I now at the table. She sat at one end and I at the other. Where to start? I was choking, and the tears rolled down my cheeks while I searched for words. "Bessie, honey, what in the world is going on?" I hadn't come to worry her but that was exactly what was happening. I took a deep breath and stifled my tears and started, "Do you know how much you mean to me, how much I love you?". I tried to look at her through my blur of tears.

She realized why I had come, I needed to say my peace in case she didn't make it. She started talking, trying to calm me. She was the eternal mama, not concerned about what was to happen to her but worried about how she needed to get her child through if God called her home. "Yes, I know how much you love me…I had a mommy too. It is scary, I know, but Bessie if I don't make it then you have to go on. It won't be easy, you will miss me. Your children need you and you will want to watch grandbabies grow. It will be hard but know I love you too! I have no regrets where my children and grandbabies are concerned, I have loved you all and life has been good to me.". I looked at her being so strong for 'her rock'. I pleaded like a child, "What will I do without you, I don't know how to go on!". I moved towards her to hold her hand. "Yes, Bessie, you do know. I showed you! I lost my mommy and I poured myself into loving my babies, you will do the same. It will hurt but you will make it. Besides, I plan on making it, let's see what God has in store." I hadn't prayed prayer B in such a long time. I wanted to pray that we would go together but, I couldn't. It would have meant leaving behind my children and I didn't want that. I had to have faith like a mustard seed and hope it would move a mountain!

The morning of surgery her family filled her room. Each time a nurse or doctor came in I could see they felt a little overwhelmed…this lady was loved a lot! It must have added some pressure to an already intense situation for them. The surgeon and anesthesiologist squeezed into the room to go over how things would happen. There would be a screen on the wall in the waiting room showing her family the stages of the procedure- pre op, surgery, closing, post op, and recovery. First, she would be taken to remove spinal fluid before surgery would begin, it would be a lengthy surgery…try not to worry, a nurse at the desk would answer questions on how things were going. After she is back in recovery, we would be allowed to see her briefly, two at a time. She would be going to ICU and he warned us upon first sight we may feel overwhelmed…she wouldn't look like herself and there would be lots of equipment on her. He wanted to prepare us, her loved ones, more so than her I think. She will not wake up the first night, this is normal to keep her sedated. A nurse will be with her at all times. "Any questions?". The only question I remember was that of my mother's. She asked, "Do you believe in God?". His response, "Yes I do." Mom, "Well that's all I need to know.".

Her vascular surgeon had told us there would be a team including a cardiologist, Dr. C, who remained her doctor for the rest of her life. Mom had the greatest doctors who really seemed to care for her. I had told Dr. C about how the family had to take her ladder away to keep her from getting on top of the roof to sweep. He remembered this and would tell his staff every time I brought her in, "This is the lady I told you about, her family took her ladder to keep her off the roof!" He loved her, he always would tell me at the end of her visit that he wished every patient of his had a family that took care of their loved ones as her family had. I would tell him it was easy, she had taken care of us and we loved her.

The surgery had been successful, she had made it! If I remember correctly it took a little over nine hours, I may be wrong though. The surgeon came out to tell us that everything went well and warned us again she would not look the same. My brother and I went in together, as soon as I seen her, I let out a small whimper. My brother patted my back and reminded me the doctor warned us. "Look how strong she is, not many could have made it, but she did.", he said to me. We both knew it was because we had prayed with her before surgery, her family and the surgeon, that and her mountain woman stubborness! I tried to find a path to her to kiss her cheek; I counted nineteen IV bags hanging from endless poles not to mention the endless monitors and equipment surrounding her bed. I laid a kiss on her cheek as did my brother, we told her she had made it and we would help her get back to her old self. I am sure she didn't hear us, but I am equally sure that each member of our family planted a kiss and whispered words of encouragement into her ear. I remember her telling Dr. C at almost every visit, after he would tell her how she was doing so well, that she was blessed to have a family that would do anything for her. We were the ones that were blessed with calling her Mom and Grandma- we knew it then, we still know it today!

She would spend so much time in ICU that she developed ICU psychosis, although not uncommon, it was terrifying for her as well as the rest of us. We would come to visit to find her restrained because she would try to pull her IV lines out or get up out of bed. She actually did pull a pic line out leaving blood everywhere as they hurried to restrain her. Sometimes she knew the loved one or friend visiting and sometimes not. One minute she would tell me she loved me and how beautiful I was. The next minute while gritting her teeth she would be saying that I was getting on her nerves and to get out. She would put up a fight with every test, wrapping her legs so tightly around her wheelchair that they couldn't budge her. The nurse actually chuckled saying, "I have never seen someone who has been through what she has and still be so strong, we had to pry her legs off that chair to take her to x-ray and watch that she didn't kick us into the next room!". She may not have been in her right mind but that strong willed mountain woman was still in there somewhere, it had been bred into her! It would be a matter of priority to get her into a room and out of ICU. She needed to see the sun rise and set to see the passage of the day and a sense of time. Her television needed to be set to channels showing current events, she needed reality to bring her back to her own mind and to us. With each visit new hallucinations would occur. She would not accept her dentures because she thought them to be poisoned. She blamed my youngest for setting fire to her house when in fact she had been the one that left a skillet on the stove thus setting fire to her kitchen. She would tell me how she had seen a van that stole her grandbabies and I needed to find the van and get them back. She spoke with such urgency and fear that if she hadn't been restrained, she would have jumped up to hunt the culprits down herself. She would see a little girl at the end of her bed; eyeing the end of her bed I asked what she was looking at. "That girl there (pointing) has been there all day but never speaks to me. I don't know why she stays there. There is a man in the bathroom wearing a dark coat and hat that peeks out at me too!". I told the imaginaries to leave and not come back. This would appease Mom until the next day when the scenario again would be repeated. I thought about Grandma and covering the freezing babies, was this how Mom was going to stay…locked in a mind that wasn't hers and me not able to find the key and free her. On one visit she told me how she now had a boyfriend that bought her all kinds of expensive jewelry and expensive clothing, whispering as if it had to be kept a secret. I asked what he looked like and she said, "There he is!", as she pointed to the television… it was President Obama! I had to laugh and reminded her that he was married; she insisted he was leaving his wife for her.

Before the surgery Mom had signed a power of attorney naming me to fill the position. I had to approve certain procedures and at the very least be kept informed. I tried to keep working at my job during the day and visit in the evenings. Some days I would just go home and call the nurse's station. She had someone in the family visiting everyday informing each other of the visit's events. I had received a call to get the okay for a blood transfusion which I gave consent for; however, days later I walked into her room as she was receiving another. I asked the nurse why hadn't I been called to give consent and she said that I had given it days prior so it was assumed that I would give it again. "That's not the point! I am to be alerted if anything changes and don't assume my consent. I know it has to be given not assumed!". Another time I came into Mom's room and asked the nurse how Mom was doing. This one said that Mom now had pneumonia; I was devastated… how much more could Mom live through? Sometimes I spent the night just so she wouldn't be restrained and I could be sure she was taking her breathing treatments. Other family members did as well but there couldn't be someone there every night. She would refuse treatments when we were not there to insist, and the restraints I am sure were placed back on as soon as we left. I was exhausted, worried, and concerned that I was losing my own mind. Mom's niece (the oldest daughter of her beloved sister) volunteered to spend a week at the hospital with Mom. It was a huge blessing to say the least. I assume the technician who was to give Mom her nightly breathing treatment had become used to having her therapy refused. She obviously didn't know Mom now had a guest for the week and would mark Mom as a refusal without even asking if she would take the treatment. My cousin had said that Mom had needed her treatment, but no one came to give her one. When I inquired, I was told she had refused it! My cousin said no one had come into the room and she had most certainly needed it. I was livid! I demanded to speak to the head nurse while my son n law contacted a friend whose wife was the CEO of the hospital. I had decided- today was the day I too would lose my mind and shit was about to hit the fan!

I paced in front of the nurse's station, thinking about a few days prior. Mom now had gout in her hip and the slightest movement caused great pain. I came into her room finding two caregivers changing her sheets, rolling her carelessly side to side with her crying out in pain. I said, "She has gout! You are hurting her!" They barely acknowledged me, I could see in Mom's eyes she was grateful I had arrived. I scanned the room and saw her untouched lunch tray. I asked if anyone had offered it, I knew she didn't have much of an appetite, but it still needed to be brought to her. "It was left here in case she decided to eat, she hasn't touched it yet.", was the response I got. I said, "How is she suppose to eat if it sits over there and she stays restrained because no one has the time to babysit her?". Waiting for an answer but getting a dumbfounded look instead! "If she eats then you will have to keep her untied or feed her! Don't sit it over there for her to look across the room at! What the hell!". They left, and I fed her! No one at the nurse's station met my gaze but I could feel their stare upon me. I know some felt sorry and some probably thought I couldn't possibly know how demanding their job was. I was not making friends to say the least! I had always treated medical staff with the utmost respect since they can control your pain and you needed them to get better. I was not feeling respectful today, I was going to whip the first ass that looked at me wrong! I was going to chew up the head nurse and then spit her out onto her sorry staff! Try me... I am the daughter of that mountain woman in the room next door, her blood flows in my veins and today this woman will show you all what an unrestrained descendent can do! Finally, I noticed heads turning slightly looking down the hallway. I turned to see a woman walking towards me, this is who I have been waiting for! Hang tough I had told myself, you are your mother's voice today! As she came closer, I could see this wasn't the first time she had walked into a battleground. She walked hurriedly to my side, her eyes showed genuine concern as she escorted me to a small private room. We sat across from each other. She said, "Tell me everything.". I sat there not knowing where to begin, so much to tell yet I didn't know what to say first. I was trembling as if I was standing in the coldest of winds. I was breaking, and I didn't want to; I had to be strong now more than ever...for Mama! She said, "Just start anywhere, it doesn't have to be at the beginning.". I opened my mouth and sobbed as I shattered into a million tiny pieces. I told her every word I have written and much more. When I said pneumonia, she stopped me. "Your mother doesn't have pneumonia!" I looked at her stunned, I described the nurse who had told me. I could tell heads were about to roll but it wasn't going to be mine. I told her about the respiratory therapist who put my mother down as a refusal without even walking into the room, she had been too busy laughing with a coworker from what my cousin had said. The therapist actually came clean and confirmed that she had marked treatment as a refusal. At the end of my ranting I told her, "If Mom doesn't get her mind back, I am going to lose mine!" This woman was not only sympathetic but assured me that Mom would get her mind back. She explained Mom had been traumatized, the surgery and the ICU psychosis were a major transition to body and mind. She will get her mind back and she will recover but it is a slow process. From then on, I was to call her directly with my concerns and she would respond asap, she was true to her word. The CEO would visit Mom and things became much better, no longer did her food sit out of reach or misinformation given. Mom started showing real progress soon after. She got her mind back and was moved to a facility to concentrate on therapy that would get her back home. Of course, she wanted to be home immediately and fought therapy out of protest of not being where she wanted to be. I just kept reminding her to do the therapy, it was the only way to get her home! Finally, almost three months after surgery, she made it home!

She never returned fully to the woman she had been prior to surgery; however, she was alive and back to carrying on conversation and making our favorite goodies! She often repeated herself or lost concentration mid sentence. She was never as strong and no longer could mow the grass. She now took naps during the day and slept in later. Little chores would wear her out. I would run her to appointments and stop on the way home to pick her up lunch. She always wanted to buy, and I wouldn't let her, I had my pay…time with my mama…priceless!

Even though the journey had been a rough ride we were thankful that God had blessed our family with more time! Roles seemed to reverse- I and my daughters took care of her medications – it had become too confusing for her. I cut her grass and pulled the weeds taking over her once well attended flowerbeds. My pay would be an ice cold diet coke to drink while sitting at the table talking about whatever was on her mind. I became the parent and she the child, I can only hope that I did as good a job as she had. I tried Mom, you left such big shoes to fill!

THE COMPLIMENT

As a young girl, while my bedroom was still upstairs, I needed no alarm clock. Every morning I would lay in bed and listen to the ritual of Dad getting ready for work. First, I would hear the water shut off from the shower and the sliding back of the curtain. I would listen for him to turn on the sink and open the medicine cabinet to retrieve his razor; I never remember my Dad having any mustache or beard, unless sick, then it was just 5 o'clock shadow. I would hear the tapping of the razor against the wall of the sink as he rinsed it after each stroke of his face. When finished, I heard him rinse his face as he blew the water away, making a snorting sound. I heard the towel rack wiggle as he dried. The best part of his routine, which was actually my favorite, was when he opened the door and stepped out. His 'Old Spice' aftershave would waft to my open door and fill my room with his scent. It was the best smell in the world! This scent, even today, takes me to a place where times were golden, where my world was perfect, I had my mom and my dad still! He would then walk to the kitchen and fill the tea kettle with water and place it back on the stove. He would fetch a cup from the cabinet and spoon from the drawer trying to be quiet as not to wake me. I was awake though, not realizing he was making a memory for me to relish way after he would be gone. The pot began to whistle, and he would snatch it up, filling his cup and measuring a heaping spoon of instant coffee to add. I would hear the clanking of the spoon against the cup as he stirred. The spoon would be placed into the sink as he walked over to the table, claiming his chair at the head of it, his spot as head of our family. His first taste would be a slow slurp, testing the heat so as not to burn his tongue. The ritual complete- time for me to rise.

Our evenings were spent watching the shows my parents had taken a liking to. 'The Lawrence Welk Show' for Dad, and 'Hee Haw' or 'The Waltons' for Mom. I think these shows reminded them of the good ole days. Dad also loved 'The Benny Hill' show but Mom didn't allow me to watch it. 'Mash' was also a favorite. We made Jiffy Pop popcorn on the stove, we stood waiting for the foil to rise, it was like a magic show. Dad eventually bought a popper shaped like a circus train car, it had spot on top where a stick of butter would be placed so the steam would butter the popcorn perfectly.

Dad handled the checkbook and wrote out the bills, Mom handed him part of her earnings and paid cash for the household stuff. This worked for them until Dad was gone. I had to show Mom how to write checks and keep her account balanced. I handled insurance claims and the paperwork that funerals bring about. My brothers, sister, and I picked out his casket...Mom chose his clothing. I took his 'Old Spice' to the funeral director who said," You won't be able to smell it, you get the smell from the sweat glands which now don't sweat.". I told him to put it on him anyway. He never started his day without it. My brothers were my Mom's biggest comfort, again I was not comfortable with this. I had my grief and loads of paperwork to keep me as busy as possible. Shortly after laying Dad to rest I had a dream. I heard him in the bathroom shaving. I crept to the open door to see his face with traces of shaving cream on his cheek as he lowered his razor to look at me. He was standing at the sink in his work pants and sleeveless undershirt. He looked worried and said to me," Bessie, tell your mother to let me go!". I left my Dad there to search out my mom, I went outside to see his navy blue casket we had buried him in lying in the yard under our crabapple tree. The soil around it was fresh and I knew she had dug it up and brought it home. I awoke and later went to Mom's and told her of my dream. "He wants you to let him go Mom,". She simply said, "I don't know how.". Neither did I.

Years after Mom's major surgery it would become necessary to take over her checkbook. She would forget to list her purchases in the ledger and it would be a mess to figure out. She would have me write her bills and mail them. I would leave her three blank checks and every day we would go over her expenditures. She was saving money too, not knowing her exact balance kept her from giving it all away. Her mail consisted of every charity known to man- I told her to pick two. She had picked Children's Hospital and Homeless Veterans. Later on, it became necessary to leave her alone as little as possible; we took turns as a family spending nights with her. She would forget her medicine or get day doses mixed up with night doses. I ran her to doctor's appointments that were plentiful. I didn't mind- we had some of our best conversations as we traveled to and from. She had stopped smoking, using an E cigarette, although I would find a lighter hidden in the bathroom...I was raising a teenager! I didn't want to see Mom getting older, but it was happening! She was more forgetful than usual, often repeating herself. She was still driving. One day, at the grocery store, Mom was backing out of her parking spot slowly and a lady made a remark that she could back faster if she put her cigarette down. Mom hollered out her window, "Bitch, bitch, bitch.", she wasn't calling her one, she was mocking her complaint. Luckily, the woman walked on. We were all becoming more concerned; however, she didn't want to give up her independence. By this time my oldest daughter and her family was living with her, a huge blessing for me. This relieved me of stopping every day after work. However, it was heartbreaking at times for my daughter. She would tell me how Mom would wake up crying out in her sleep, she had been dreaming of her mommy, daddy, and sister. She awoke thinking them all to still be alive and my daughter had to explain that they all had gone to heaven. Mom would cry if it was the first time hearing it. It really took a toll on my child to see her grandma in such pain. This played out many times.

Mom also developed health problems and now had to be weighed every day. If she gained three pounds she would have to be given Lasix and when back to normal the med would have to be stopped. She had difficulty making it to the bathroom, so I put a portable potty beside her bed. She felt awful when I changed her sheets, took her laundry home, or mowed the grass. She just wasn't strong enough anymore. I had to face that Mom was old. Her hands took on the look of my grandmother's hands that I had remembered playing with. We cooked anything she wanted, and she no longer wanted to ride with me to the store, now she just gave me a list. My oldest daughter moved out and my youngest moved in. I was back to stopping every day or at least calling on my way home. Mom and I had a long talk about how it was time to stop driving. I told her if she broke down, had an accident, or got lost I would not be able to leave work to get to her. Everybody in our family worked, my daughter living with her was working second shift…no one would be available. She reluctantly agreed. I took the keys home with me. Mom had a cell phone but could never figure it out. My daughter wrote on the back of her home phone the numbers to reach us. Everyone stopped by to check on her and she would pitifully tell them how I had taken her keys away. I didn't know how else to keep her safe, she had agreed, but was now 'throwing me under the bus'. It made me feel horrible, but that was not her intent, I think she just wanted someone's attention.

I stopped by one afternoon after work to find her sitting in her green glider at the table; the expression on her face told me something was wrong. "What's going on? You look so sad." I asked. "I am so lonely Bessie. I have no energy- I still feel like I am sixteen on the inside but sometimes it's all I can do to get up out of this chair. I sit here and think about leaving Mommy when she needed me home. I think about how my Daddy was sick and I didn't take care of him. I think how all my brothers and sisters are gone. I am of no use, I have become a burden to my kids." I listened and then I said, "Mom, how can you be lonely?". My daughter would leave for work and two or three hours later I would be there, unless, someone else was stopping by. I called her every evening before she went to bed, tucking her in by phone and my daughter would be there soon after she fell asleep. "Mom, you were a wonderful daughter and sister, they wouldn't want you to be sad.". For the first time in my life my mother would explain what loneliness really is. "You can be in a room full of people and be lonely Bessie. My thoughts take me to a place I long to be, a time when I was young and with Mommy. I miss Home and all those I grew up with. I miss where I began!". I cried for my own mom, I would have given or done anything for her; the one thing she wanted was to go Home again and the only way to get there was in memories. Instead of home healthcare I had a friend stay with Mom a few hours a day to keep her mind occupied. The friend would tell me that Mom would talk a little while and then go nap two or three hours at a time. I asked Mom why she would want to nap so much with company around. "Well honey, I'll tell ya, I try to stay awake, but I stay tired. When I sleep, I see Mommy and my sister standing in a dirt road, they are dressed in white gowns and look young again. They look so beautiful. They are waiting for me Bessie; I may see eighty, but I won't make it to eighty-one." I said, "Mom, you can tell them your bags ain't packed!". Her dream scared me, but I made myself believe it was just a dream and not a premonition. Once again God was talkin' and I wasn't listening!

Shortly after the dream conversation, I had stopped up to mow the grass, it was autumn, but the weather had kept the grass growing. Finished, I went in to collect my diet coke and sit a spell. She told me how her shoulder ached, and I got up to massage it. I was concerned about pneumonia, but she had just recently had a chest x-ray. She thought she had slept wrong, so I accepted that, probably right. I got up to leave and just before I rounded the hallway to the stairs, she called me back. I turned around at the corner to see her smiling where she sat in her chair. "Bessie, you remind me of my mommy." I was shocked, honored, and ashamed all at the same time. "Mom, that is the greatest compliment I have ever had but I don't deserve it. You don't know me as good as you think you do, and I sure can't begin to measure up to Grandma!". She stopped me from continuing, "Now listen here my lady, there isn't a thing I ask that you don't do. I bet I know more than you think I do. I have seen you so tired that you wish you could drop in the bed, but you come here to take care of me and my house. I see the sweat pour down your face and not once have you complained, that's the same way Mommy was." I went to her and knelt down, I gave her cheek a kiss and melted into her hug. She whispered about how sorry she was to be such a burden, I whispered back, "You are not my burden, you are my mommy. Thank you for thinking I am worthy of such a compliment!". I left, and on my way home I cried; the tears were not about what she had said, I cried because she thought me to be close to perfect and I knew how wrong she was!

PACKING HER BAGS

It was now November and Mom would soon be eighty. My daughter had taken her for a flu shot since that season would soon be approaching. She once again started to complain of pain in her shoulder which I attributed to the recent flu shot. She had recently seen her doctor and everything had been good. She now also had been seeing an oncologist after having several bad nose bleeds. I'm not sure why she was referred to an oncologist but once again she had charmed another doctor. Her last visit before being released of his care fell on her birthday, I joked about it being her birthday and she stopped me, telling me no one needs to know how old she is. My mother never cared about age, I thought it strange that she did now. The nurse took her blood pressure and it was high, it hadn't been high in a very long time. She recommended that we keep an eye on it and to follow up with her primary care physician. I called his office when we returned home; they could see her in three weeks and told me if her pressure became higher to take her to emergency but that she would probably be fine with taking the Lasix for a couple of days. That night the family came to her house to celebrate her birthday, she seemed happy and content.

Her blood pressure seemed better too! I never took any pictures that night, I guess I forgot. I wish I had thought to do so. My mother had said she would make it to eighty and she had, Happy Birthday Mom!

It was now early December and I called Sunday morning to tell Mom I was coming over later to fix her a fresh pork steak from a hog that had recently been butchered. She asked that I stop and buy some asparagus to go with it, "You know it's good for fighting all kinds of cancer!". I picked up her request along with a fruity vegetable salad from the salad bar. As I cooked, she reminded me to only steam the asparagus for a little while so as not to lose the good stuff that fights cancer. I put the unused vegetable into her fridge for another meal. She ate good and seemed to really enjoy her meal.

The next day at work turned out to be a long one; it was not only Monday, the heaviest day of the week, but we were in the holiday season. I needed to pick up my youngest daughter's children after work by 6 o'clock. I left work at six, so I called to let the sitter know that I was on my way. I passed Cedar Drive as I dialed Mom's number, I wanted to check in and let her know I had to pick up the babies. She answered the phone saying, "I prayed you would call, I have been sitting on the kitchen floor for four hours!" I immediately turned around while she explained that her grandson had come to visit and had no sooner walked out the door she had fallen. "I yelled for him but he couldn't hear me." I called the sitter as I drove down Cedar and she assured me to take my time, just take care of your mama.

I parked and ran upstairs to her. "Why didn't you call me, my number is on the back of the phone?" I asked. Thank God the phone had been lying next to her, she thought it was the t.v. remote. She said, "I yelled for those kids out in the yard to come help me, but I guess they couldn't hear me." There were no kids in the backyard. I knew her mind was playing tricks on her. My daughter's dog lay there the entire time next to her as she petted her. "This dog sure is good to me, bless her heart.". I asked if she hurt anywhere and assured me she was not hurt. I scooted a kitchen chair next to her and told her to hold onto my arms as I lifted her to the chair. Her legs had become numb and would not bend and she would start to slide as I placed her on the chair. I eased her back onto the floor and called my oldest daughter who I knew was on her way home from work. I explained what had happened and that I needed her help, I also asked her to call the sitter again as I was going to be really late. As we waited for help, Mom apologized, "I peed myself, I couldn't get up, so I just went…I'm sorry Bessie.". I told her not to be sorry, we would have her up and cleaned in no time, no need to be upset about it. My daughter arrived and we got her sitting, then standing, and finally walking. We cleaned her and dressed her, then cleaned the floor. We checked for bruising but found no discoloration. My daughter said for me to go get the babies and she would stay with her. As I drove, I thought to call my daughter and ask her to take Mom's blood pressure. She did; it was sky high. I then called my youngest brother and told him what had happened, I told him about the blood pressure. He said for my daughter to call the squad and he would meet Mom at the hospital. I told him I could relieve him at 11p.m. when the babies would be picked up. He said no that he would stay and when he knew more he would call. I called him a couple of times before falling asleep but there wasn't any news yet. I worried that Mom once again would have pneumonia, it would be so hard for her to bounce back. I awoke at 3:18 a.m. and checked my phone, I had not missed a call, so I sent a text to my brother. I knew his daughter and her boyfriend was there with him too. I thought about texting her too. My brother called at 3:30 a.m. and I could hear that he was choked up- I thought,' Oh it is pneumonia!', but he said, "Mom has lung cancer!" My mind was racing as I felt the tears coming, how could I have missed this? The weakness, the sore shoulder, high blood pressure…I had given the flu shot, arthritis, and sleeping wrong the blame! She had a sizeable mass in her right lung. My brother told me that she knew and all she said was this, "I've done this to myself, you will have to tell your brother and sister, I can't.". The wind was knocked out of me as I tried to comprehend, and I realized she must have suspected this…the dream, the asparagus, the loneliness…all signs that maybe something was going on but just not wanting to admit it to us. She had found out the morning of December 9th, the day her beloved sister had died years ago of lung cancer!

I don't remember who I told first but I do know I called my oldest brother's house right before 6 a.m. My sister answered the phone and said he had already left for work. I told her I needed to talk to her and she said to come on, she would have coffee ready. The last time I had cried at their table was over their daughter, this time it would be for our mom. I left her after a couple of hours with the awful task of telling my brother and her children. I was faced with telling my family and friends. We all knew what we couldn't say, we were going to lose her!

I called off work and went to the hospital. From then, until she died, we never said the 'C' word to each other. I stopped at the gift shop and bought her a snowman hat; figuring it would keep her head warm if she chose not to wear her wig. Her wig lie on the floor and her little body was curled up at the end of the bed. She awoke and smiled, glad to see me. I asked her if she wanted her wig and she replied, "Throw that old thing in the drawer!". I did. I showed her the hat, which made her laugh, and I put it on her. Friend came by to see her and support me. We talked but not about cancer. I was her power of attorney and she said for me to do what needed to be done. The days became a whirlwind and I don't remember the order of things taking place, I just know what did.

She would need an oncologist and the hospital was going to set her up with one. I thought about the one we had seen for her nose bleeds and asked for him to be contacted, I felt God had put him in her life for a reason, done! The doctor that admitted her told us she had small cell cancer which is aggressive and Mom's mass was sizeable. They could be aggressive with chemo, but it would not save her but may buy time. She would still die just maybe later than the month they assumed she had left. My brothers and I talked with our spouses but ultimately, I would have to sign off on, all decisions had to be made quickly. There would be no chemo. I came into her room while my brother was visiting, the oncologist I had requested came in to see her. He told her that she would be moving to the fourth floor and they would begin an intense round of chemo the next morning, I shook my head no and looked at my brother. Obviously, he had not received the message of our decision. My brother asked to speak with him in the hallway. He told him we had decided not to do the chemo, we knew it would not save her and we didn't want her last days to be sick and in pain. "What would you do if this was your mom?", my brother would ask. The doctor said, "I would say no to the chemo, she probably wouldn't make it through the first round. If she were my mother, I would take her home and be with her. You are making the right choice." The doctor walked back into the room and told Mom she would not be moving to the fourth floor that the chemo would be of no use, "Is there anything I can do for you?" he asked. Mom said, "Find me a cure." He politely replied, "I wish I had one to give you." He then recommended hospice care and would send someone to talk to us about options. A lady from hospice, I believe it to be Thursday, took me to a small waiting area and explained about home care or facility care, I chose home care- I knew Mom would want her last days to be inside her own familiar surroundings and she was already anxious to go home. I asked, "How long does my mom have?". She told me maybe two weeks, but it was more than likely a few days. I couldn't understand how in just a few days it had went from a month to, now I am being told, possibly days. She explained if Mom had made it through the first chemo, and that was a mighty big if, that we may be lucky enough to get the month. Hospice care would mean taking her off her routine meds and she would be put on meds to keep her out of pain and more relaxed. Choosing neither chemo or hospice would mean a slower and much more painful death. I felt sick, decisions had to be made so fast, I chose the hospice care. Forgive me God, was this what you would want me to do or am I stepping on your toes? If I have made the wrong decision then blame me, but please let it be the right one for her. I was given numbers to call to order a hospital bed and other equipment necessary for her care, I did, everything would be there at her home by Sunday. Sunday she could come home and stay until God would take her back home with him. I signed the paperwork, and she handed me another paper explaining it was a 'DNR', no extreme measures...no saving Mom if her heart stopped beating. She handed me the pen and I looked at my brother beside me, I turned back to the paper and signed my name. All I could think was her bones were too fragile for CPR and I didn't want her bouncing back and forth between life and death. I didn't take it lightly, but I had to sign it quickly; otherwise, I never would have.

I went to work on Friday telling them I would not be returning until my mother no longer needed me, we all knew what that meant. I wanted to be with her, as did all her family. The hospital had been trying to reach me that day, but my phone was acting up and by the time I figured it out I was already on my way there. I called my sister who told me when she arrived to visit with Mom; things had gotten pretty hairy. Mom had three nurses in her room trying to coax her back into bed. Mom had gotten out of bed and was demanding to go home, she was pointing out the window showing in which direction her home was. She was mad, and they were scared of her, she even had one blocked from leaving the room. My sister stepped in at the right time and tried to calm her. Mom finally did sit back onto the bed, but she was still demanding to go home. I got there to find her glaring up at me, she scared me a little too! I told her that she would be going home on Sunday. "Why do I have to wait, I want to go home NOW!". I told her that we had a bed coming to be placed in the living room so she wouldn't have to climb the steps. "Well I better go home Sunday or I will call a taxi to take me!". The mountain woman had emerged with all her strength in tow, she was scary and amusing at the same time- it was good to see our little mountain woman making a stand, but it would be her last. Saturday found her much calmer when Friend and I came to visit. We talked about God and how he is always good. She was handing out motherly advice and told me never to cry over material things. I knew what she was hinting at, she didn't want me feeling guilty about selling or losing the homeplace. She then looked at me and said, "I want to be cremated." I knew this is not what she wanted, I had known it all my life; she was looking to make it easier for her family financially! I leaned in and said, "I could never do that to you!". She shook her head at me and I said, "Everything is fine!". I was letting her know that she wasn't leaving us with a burden.

Mom left the hospital and arrived home by ambulance on Sunday. We made her comfortable in the hospital bed that sat in the middle of her living room. She would wear an attends, (adult diaper), unable to walk up the stairs to the bathroom, unable to walk or even get out of bed. She lay there happily while family surrounded her with love and attention. My sister had made Mom blackberry dumplings and she ate a few bites. Her appetite wasn't good which had always been a sign of fluid building up in her body. Mom would likely die of something other than the cancer itself since she had been taken off all her regular medications. A hospice nurse visited to go over her care with us. She showed me how and how much morphine and ativan to give when the time came. Our family was standing there listening, and I saw Mom's frightened face, "What's this for? I don't want to be drunk. What are you doing to me?". I was scared too! I didn't want to mess up. I told her the meds were for pain and anxiety, we wouldn't be drugging her up. The nurse knew I was scared and said that a full- time nurse would be coming as soon as one was available. I guess there was many people saying goodbyes and the need for hospice was in high demand. It was good to have her home and she seemed to be doing well. I lay on the couch that night in case she needed anything, she seemed a little restless. At one point before family had left, she got my attention. "Bessie, I see my mommy and daddy in this room." She was in her right mind and I knew she was actually seeing them. I said, "Well, of course they would be here, they are here to take care of their girl.". She seemed so happy knowing they were there with her.

2:30 a.m. Monday morning our hospice nurse came. She was a quiet lady but very nice. The nurses would work 12 hour shifts; the last thirty minutes would be going over notes with the next nurse coming on duty. The nurses were very kind and they seemed to be there as our support system as well. The meds had to be accounted for at the beginning of each shift, thank God I never had to administer any med. The morphine started in a small dose and made Mom itchy. My youngest bought coconut oil and would rub her down with it which seemed to ease the itch. Ativan was also given to help with this. Mom's leg began hurting pretty severely, I knew it was gout…we had to be extra gentle changing her. Even when sleepy from the morphine, she would moan if that leg was touched. I asked the day nurse on Monday if they could send a pastor to pray over Mom, he would come the next day.

Tuesday morning came, and I fed Mom McDonalds biscuits and gravy, she had always liked their gravy. She only took a couple of bites and a few sips of diet coke. This would be her last meal. She was now asleep more than awake; I am sure this was because of the morphine. She still moaned while changing her and I began to think a catheter may be a good idea. I talked to the nurse about it and she thought it a good idea. I knew Mom would not like this, but it was the only way to stop the changings. Mom was always very private, and she would not have been happy to get catheterized in her living room; I just could think of no other way to keep from hurting her. I also told the nurse that I couldn't be present; I knew it was the right thing to do but I could not be a part of it. I had a doctor appointment later that day, so it would be done while I was gone. I felt like I was deceiving her, I just wanted to minimize the episodes of moving her leg. The nurse said she was going to bathe Mom and I told her I would help. I wrapped my arm around the base of her neck, supporting her head. I used my other arm to hold her so her back could be washed. I held her close to my face, kissing her forehead. When the nurse had finished with her back, I started to lay her back down. I felt Mom grip me and she said, "Take care Bessie." I said, "I will Mom.". I knew what she meant; take care of the family. Don't let my death cause everyone to scatter. Family is everything. Many times she had told me that during the end of days families will fall apart. She wanted me to assure her that I would not let that happen to hers. These would be her last words to me; she may have been able to hear us, but she no longer spoke or opened her eyes.

The pastor arrived and prayed over Mom. He then turned his attention to me, "How do You feel about losing your Mom? Are you sad? What will you miss most?" He kept on and on while I looked at him like he was a moron. First of all, I knew Mom heard every word he said. Secondly, I did not ask for counselling! I answered his questions with questions. "How would you feel? Wouldn't you be sad?". I think he got the hint and when I was surveyed on hospice care I gave everyone gold stars but him. I had asked for prayer, not for someone to psycho analyze me.

People were stopping by right and left to see Mom- my friends, people she had once worked with, friends of family, neighbors.... So many loved her. I went on to my appointment while my youngest promised to help the nurse with cathing her grandma. I felt guilty, but I would have made it worse. After my appointment, I called my daughter to ask how it went. She said grandma did holler out, "Now you stop that!". She had used her last hurrah in protest, not because of the catheter but because her privacy was being invaded. She would no longer need to be changed, no leg moving, and that was the goal- mission accomplished. I'm sorry Mom, I just wanted you to be comfortable. I told my daughter I would be home soon; I was going to stop at the store across the way to just look for a couple of Christmas gifts.

I went over to the store, it was dusk, I wasn't staying long. I stood in the toy aisle, staring but not looking at anything. I called a man I knew from my mail route and who I knew did some preaching at the church across the street from my house. I called him while standing there and told him about my mother. I asked if he would pastor her service and come to Mom's to talk with our family. He said yes to both. I left the store without making a purchase. As I walked out, I looked around for my vehicle. It was now dark making it more difficult. I searched up and down the rows closest to the entrance of the store. I know I hadn't parked far away. I couldn't find it. I called both of my daughters separately while each tried to calm me. I was in a panic bordering an anxiety attack. I stood there while people drove or walked by. A light snow started to fall, and the wind picked up making me shake. "I can't find it; I have looked in every row. I have to get back to Mom! Why didn't I just cancel this stupid appointment? Why did I stop at this stupid store?" I cried into the phone. As they were trying to calm me, all I could think was that my mom was dying, and I can't get to her. I can't find my car to get back to her. They assured me Grandma is fine. Use your panic button on your key fob… I did. Nothing. I walked the rows again hitting the unlock button on my key. Finally, I seen the lights come on; I had found it. It was close to the entrance and I must have passed it several times. The snow stopped. I sat in the vehicle and cried. I took a deep breath and asked God to get me home; I still have no recollection of the drive back to Mom's- I just know by the grace of God I had made it and she was still alive.

Wednesday morning the nurse explained that hospice care would pull out of the home after 72 hours if the patient had no change; in other words, if said patient wasn't actively dying. I was terrified because that would mean I would have to administer the morphine. She assured me if there was any change with Mom all

I had to do was call and they would send the first available nurse out. I added it up, we would have care until 2:30 a.m. the next morning…less than 24 hours. She also suggested each family member take some time to talk to Mom alone, she would be able to hear us, and it would be comforting to her. We each took our turn. My stepdaughter was due to fly in from Texas on Saturday, Mom always worried about her flying. She cried out her name twice that day in her comatose state. I called my stepdaughter and held the phone to Mom's ear, I also called her beloved sister's oldest daughter and did the same. Her oldest grandson would have to leave that day to return to work out of state. I felt sorry for him most of all that day. His Grandma had been more like a mother to him, helping his dad raise him after his parents divorced. I didn't know who would be there in Mom's final moments, but I knew he would not, and he knew it too! His tears fell like rain and tears seeped through her closed eyes. That was her boy! I know she wanted to tell him it would be okay, but she couldn't. As he walked out the door, knowing he had seen his grandma for the last time, I went to him and hugged him, "You're her boy! She loves you!". I hated to see him go and be alone to deal with his hurt but there was nothing any of us could do. I just prayed that God would watch over him. I went to Mom and wiped the tears. I leaned down and told her what I had told him. "He knows you love him, and I promise his Daddy will take care of him. I love him too. He will hurt but we will make sure he's okay. I'll take care, I promise.". Later, I told Mom that God would take care of her, "If God takes care of the little bird, surely he takes care of you.", repeating what Friend had told me. I relived her memories of the one room schoolhouse and how she had gotten out of that vaccination. I then said, "When you get to heaven you are going to have a headful of hair and when I get there I will be thin, won't we be a pair? I love you Mom. Thank you for being my Mom, I am blessed! Save a place for me!". It was getting late and one by one the family started to go, giving goodnight kisses with the promise of being back the next day. My sister n law was studying for her bar exam at the kitchen table, she was the last to leave. My daughter, my niece, and I were left. A new nurse was on duty, one that had not been there before. It was barely past 12:30 a.m., two more hours and she would be told to leave, thanks to medicare guidelines. My daughter went downstairs to lie down and stay with her sleeping baby. I headed upstairs to lie down with my oldest grandbaby who was already fast asleep. I thought about how my own grandson had cried earlier and Mom could hear him. Mom had lifted her arm as if to hold him- always the comforter- and my daughter placed him next to her in her arm. I started to drift when my niece ran up the stairs to tell me Mom's breathing had changed. This had happened several times throughout the day, so I told her it had been a normal thing that day; I wasn't impressed with this nurse, but I really had no reason not to be. My niece screamed," Aunt Bess, NOW!' I jumped out of bed and ran to the top of the stairs, I told my niece to go get my daughter. I started handing out orders to call everyone as I fidgeted with my phone to make calls too. I sat to my Mom's right, my daughter at her left, and my niece at her feet and legs. The nurse had been right about her breathing changing. Her breaths were longer and when she inhaled, her bottom jaw would drop and then click back up. The nurse said, "She is gone.". My daughter said, "No she isn't.". Mom took another breath and I leaned to her ear as I held her hand and said, "If you see your mommy, run!". Her breath stopped. The nurse again said that Mom was gone. I put my head to her chest, then my cheek to her mouth. I checked for a pulse... she was gone but I couldn't believe it. I expected a gasp, a fight for breath, something. She just stopped and ran! She died at 1:32 a.m., one hour before hospice would leave and I would fearfully have to step in. She had waited for her family to leave, go to bed, just be somewhere else while she grabbed her packed bags to leave. She didn't want to be a burden, although I had told her so many times she wasn't! The rest of the calls were made to call back the family that had just left a short time earlier. Her grandson had just pulled on to his jobsite when he got the call. I called my husband who hurried to me. I waited for everyone to come back as I washed my mother's face. I took the little sponges, that the last couple of days had been used to keep her mouth moist, and tried to remove the foam gathering in her mouth. I was lost, I didn't know what to do. The nurse called an RN who would come and call the time of death; I already knew that. Family had started coming in, I went and sat in my car. I called the funeral home so they could come claim my mama. I sat there and wondered why I had told her to run, I should have said stay! It was happening so fast that I didn't get to think it through. She was waiting for the word and I had given it to her.

Two people from the funeral came in with a stretcher and her granddaughters and I placed her on it. We then covered her with her mommy's quilt. I walked with the workers and watched them place her in the back of the vehicle. I watched as they pulled out of her driveway. I watched until the brake lights disappeared. I watched as she took her last trip down Cedar Drive! I stood there at the end of the driveway, looking for a sign I guess, that she had made it to those waiting on the dirt road in her dreams. My oldest brother came out and stood with me; we smoked a cigarette as we talked. I looked up at the sky and three bright stars appeared. She had made it! I blew them kisses and went back inside. My husband had made it there and I leaned into him to relieve my stress and hurt, he had pretty much lost his wife who had went to live at her mother's. He never once complained, he understood I had been where I needed to be. Mom always said, "God will give you your heart's desires!". He had given me the husband, the parents, the family, and friends I had desired. "I tell you Bessie, God is good all the time!". Yes mama, He is!

GOODBYE MY LADY

The arrangements were made. The casket picked out. The music chosen; each of us choosing a song. The photos were being picked through while the memories they brought back became a source of comfort. Verses, flowers, cemetery…all details seen to. I handed her clothes to the funeral director. I had bought her a white sweater for Christmas weeks ago or maybe it was a lifetime ago. She would wear this with her brown slacks that still fit. A tight fitting undershirt instead of a bra, bras had hurt her recently. Christmas booties on her feet, black with colorful snowflakes. I handed over her wig, she would probably want it on for the viewing. I had thought about having her buried with her mommy's quilt that rode with her to the funeral home. My brother talked me out of that idea. He said, "She would want you to have it and you are going to need it. I think you'll regret having it buried, keep it for yourself." I am glad he changed my mind. I would roll it long ways and snuggle it at night, burying my head and tears in it. My husband never asked why a rolled up quilt separated us, he knew. I thought I would eventually share it, giving each a turn. I am sorry, I won't share it. I still need it at times and I am choosing to be selfish. Giving it up would be giving her up again and I can't do it again.

My husband, Friend, step daughter and I went early to set up the pictures and momentos before the family viewing would begin. My husband and Friend carried the items into the room where my first best friend lay; I stayed outside the door. Yes Mom, I am here... I just need a minute. Friend finished assembling the items brought. She came to me and told me Mom looked beautiful. The music we had picked came on over the speakers as I went to spend time by myself with my mom. The funeral director shut the doors behind me. I walked to her wishing I could wake her. I told her about the sweater and I hoped she liked it. I thanked her for the millions of things I took for granted. I asked for forgiveness for making her worry, for mistakes made, and if I had made the wrong choices for her during the last nine days. I pulled out a tube of her lipstick I had hidden in my pocket. I spread it thickly over my lips. I bent over her and kissed her forehead, leaving the imprint of my kiss. Now she could take my kisses with her. The hymn, 'Walk Through the Garden', played over the speaker and I sang it to her. She had told me many years ago that I should sing 'The Rose' at her funeral and I had said no. "Well why not?" she had asked. "Because I won't feel like singing, I will have lost my Mom!". I stood there an orphan. That is the only way to describe it. I may have been a grown woman, but I had lost the people that had brought me into the world. They had been my everything growing up. They were the ones I turned to for love, understanding, praise, forgiveness. Then there would be one, and now, none. I felt the loneliness she had spoke of. I had nowhere to turn, nowhere to go…I had been left behind, I was an orphan.

Her sons and some of the grandchildren wore red nail polish on their pinky fingers, giving tribute to the 'milking your mouse' era! Friend placed a bible in her casket as family placed charms, jewelry, and trinkets to be buried with her. So many people came that I don't know if I got to greet everyone. I stood at her casket as my oldest grandbaby came and stood beside me. She asked me what will happen to Grandma and why do we bury the body? I told her that people are like eggs. The good stuff is on the inside but the shell is no longer needed once we get the good stuff. God took the good stuff to heaven with Him and the body is the shell left behind, it's no longer needed. She will be perfect in heaven. Her shell is buried because she no longer needs it, she isn't in there anymore." Her mother came up and whispered, "You want to know a secret? Grandma is wearing Christmas booties." Both of these revelations seemed to make her happy.

It had been an exhausting day and I looked forward to time with the quilt, snuggled against me. "Goodnight Mom, I miss you already!"

The morning of her service had arrived, just a few short weeks ago I had a mother who wasn't dying, or at least I didn't know it. I thought about a conversation we had days before, when she had first came home from the hospital. "Pretty soon I will be 33 again.". I didn't know what she meant. "That is the age Jesus died on the cross. We will all be 33 in heaven." I asked, "What about all the babies, your grandchildren, the old people who have passed? How will people know who's who?". "The hearts will know one another.", was her reply. She never told me if she had read that in the Bible or what had made her believe this. I was talking to one of the hospice nurses about visible signs to look for when time was getting close. She was talking about how many of her patients had mentioned that they would be 33 in heaven. I was shocked, I told her Mom had just told me this too. I told her I had asked how everyone would recognize each other and before I could finish the nurse would say, "The hearts would know each other.".

The pastor gave a sermon on the virtuous woman. Mom's oldest granddaughter and I, gave the eulogies. She was representing those who knew her as Grandma and I would speak on my brothers and my behalf. Her speech took me back to Sunday morning breakfast, memories of how youthful my Mom always seemed to be. The silly things she would say, the love she gave in even the smallest things she did. It was beautiful! To be her grandchild was a beautiful thing; to be her child was too!

People lined up to say their last goodbye; I waited for everyone to exit. The funeral director came to me rolling up a small paper. He said on this paper was listed the names of her family, all she belonged to. There is a slot on the outside of the casket where this is placed; he had a hard time rolling it small enough to fit. There were so many family members it had made the paper much thicker than he was used to. I walked with him as he placed it the slot. He asked if I wanted to help with the casket before wheeling it out to the hearse. "Yes." He placed a crank into the side of the casket and as I cranked her head lowered. We tucked her in; before closing the lid, I asked him to remove her wig. I put it in a bag and brought it home. It had been a constant reminder that her glory had been stolen and now God had given it back. She no longer needed it. "Throw it in a drawer.", she had once said, so I did. We closed the lid and escorted her outside where her pallbearers awaited. At the cemetery another prayer was said. Friend had brought red balloons for family to release- red was always her favorite color. The funeral director handed me a bag with the guestbook, thank you cards, etc... in it. He asked if I wanted the video from her service posted on their website. I asked if Mom would be visible in the video? He answered yes; I told him no. Mom did not believe in photographing the dead to have someone gawking at the pictures for years to come. It was done! We left the cemetery, taking only memories with us.

BAND AID

It was just a matter of days before her house too began to die. The well went dry, the fridge stopped working, the oil ran out in the oil drum and by Spring the cooling had stopped working too! As my sister would say, "It's mistress had died and it had lived to serve her.". Her belongings were divided among us. No greed took over, we all had things to treasure. I took her pajamas and some of her shirts to the Christmas gathering for her grandkids to have. The extra clothes were given to the pastor's church for the needy. The remainder was sold in a yard sale and we used the money to have one more round of Angilo's pizza that we ate it in her yard. The home would go into foreclosure, I couldn't make payments and fix all the things falling apart. She had told me not to cry over material things, but I did. Just as she longed for her childhood home, I would yearn for mine. I still do. I felt guilty leaving the unmowed grass behind, the driveway where the pine needles gathered, and the flowerbeds she had planted everywhere- would soon be taken over by weeds. Leaving the kitchen window was the hardest for me. Looking through it was like looking into heaven. I would watch my dad sit at the picnic table under the walnut tree. I could see Mom on the mower, stopping under the window asking me to bring her a diet coke with lots of ice. I saw Dad standing at the pool watching his babies swim and splash. I saw our neighbor's coming over to hang around until dark. I see Dad building the gazebo I would marry in. I see Mom carrying Dad a cup of coffee while he read the newspaper. I saw my children play with their cousins and my grandbabies hunt Easter eggs. I watch my brother paint his car and play his music too loud. I hear the clank of the horseshoes and my brothers laughing at Dad's jokes. I see Mom standing at the grill as my brother sneaks past to drop a piece of ice down the back of her shirt. "You better run honey!", I can hear her say. I had seen heaven through a kitchen window!

I went to the auction the day she was bartered away. I waited for her new owners afterwards. I told them who I was and how I had messed up and lost her. I wished them the love I had known there and of course, I cried. I wasn't just crying over material things; I was crying over everything!

Whoever said 'Time heals all wounds" has never known true grief. It ranks up there with, 'I know how you feel'. You don't know how I feel, you may know grief, but you don't know mine. I don't know yours! Grief is a bundle of things missed, people loved, memories shared, guilt and regret. No two peoples are the same! Time, it will slowly make you get up and carry on. It will allow you to laugh again, love, but it will never allow you to be the same. Time will not heal the wound made by grief. It will place a band aid on it. Sometimes you will think yourself to be fine and then it is unexpectedly ripped from your skin. It hurts! Maybe you will be fortunate enough that a scab will form. Then something will cause you to pick at it. A memory, a song on the radio, her handwriting on a piece of paper you thought was trash. The scab flakes off and the bleeding starts all over again; it never seems to be able to form a scar. The wound waits for the next time you will reopen it. Time can be cruel; the hourglass sits where you can't see it. The glass never tips to it's side allowing things to slow, it never tips to give you a few more grains. It continues, with no regard to your heartache. Time does not heal all wounds, it is just a band aid at best!

Sometimes as I drive to work, I talk to her as if she rides next to me. I tell her what is going on in my life, ask for advice, or just tell her I miss her. I look up at the sky and search for the star I think to be her. I sing to her. I blow kisses and imagine hugs. When I can't sleep, I pray. When I still can't sleep, I shut my eyes and imagine pulling into her driveway. I turn the handle of the door and enter. I walk up the stairs and listen to the creak on the third step. I walk through the kitchen and sneak a peak at the kitchen window. I round the corner to the hallway that leads to her bedroom. I see her sitting on the edge of the bed watching her show. She looks over at me, "Well, there's my girl.", as she pats the bed for me to come sit next to her. I lay my head on her shoulder, I tell her whatever is on my mind......I fall asleep. Time cannot heal this...a band aid at best.

MISSING YOU

As the flower misses the sun, waiting for a new day that has not begun, and all has been said and done,... I miss you!

As the lightening beckons the thunder, in a night sky full of wonder, alone with my thoughts to ponder,... how I miss you!

As my heart yearns to mend, mourning the loss of my best friend, waiting for sadness to finally end,... but I miss you!

While I journey to my home, I see the path I use to roam, to find you sitting with others or alone,... telling me, "I missed you!"

Just as the desert looks for the rain, I need to stroll Memory Lane, so I can feel your hug again,... and not have to miss you!

One day we will reunite, and all will be set right, and I will hold you with such delight,... and I will never again miss you!

Upon my last word of honor, I will always love and miss you!

CPSIA information can be obtained
at www.ICGtesting.com
Printed in the USA
BVHW070946250319
543611BV00008B/150/P

9 781796 021011